OFF ON A
WILD CABOOSE
CHASE . . . .

OFF ON A WILD CABOOSE CHASE . . . .

True Adventures, Folklore, and a Farewell Tribute to the Old Train Caboose by a Writer Who Lives Aboard One

ADOLF HUNGRY WOLF

CANADIAN ROCKIES

1988

WILLIAM MORROW AND COMPANY, INC.

New York

Library of Congress Cataloging-in-Publication Data

Hungry Wolf, Adolf.
Off on a wild caboose chase : true adventures, folklore, and a farewell tribute to the old train caboose by a writer who lives aboard one / Adolf Hungry Wolf.
p.   cm.
ISBN 0-688-07752-8
1. Cabooses (Railroads)   I. Title.
TF485.H86 1989
835'.32—dc19   88-13091
CIP

Printed in the United States of America

First Edition

1 2 3 4 5 6 7 8 9 10

BOOK DESIGN BY BERNARD SCHLEIFER

This book is dedicated to all those who've
ridden in cabooses and all those who own them

Acknowledgments

The author extends thanks for caboose rides to the following
individuals and railways:

- Jack Anderson and Harold Borovec, Mount Rainier Scenic
  Railroad
- David Carr, Greater Winnipeg Water District Railway
- Martin Lypka, CP Rail
- N. L. Mills, Algoma Central Railway
- Dwight Smith, Conway Scenic Railway

Thanks also to VIA Rail Canada for occasional help with
transportation; James A. Brown and Don Denlinger for caboose
accommodations; Bob Henry for the collection of old *Railroad
Magazines*; and Brian Clarkson for use of his photo darkroom.
Thanks to countless railroaders for being friendly and hospitable
to my son and me in our travels.

Contents

CHAPTER ONE

Train in the Night

There's a certain something about a train
That does things to me I can't explain.
A whistle, a roar—and a streak of light
Goes plunging headlong into the night,
Hurling itself over gleaming trails
Marked out by the headlights upon the rails.
Just a "whish" and it's passed me, front to rear,
And I'm watching the markers disappear.

There's an aching something, away inside,
That's longing to ride, and ride and ride—
With the rattle of gravel against a tie,
And the clackety-clack as the poles whiz by;
And the musical toll of a crossing-bell
Flung back on the wind, as we race pellmell
Toward some vague, far place in the inky black—
Ah, it's lonely here by the railroad track!

—WILLIS CAIRNES

He paused momentarily in the snow, savoring the cold air's icy tingle on the hairs inside his nostrils. The mountains all around him were hidden by swirling flakes blowing down from the north. It was nearly night; hunger gnawed at his empty insides. Zipping up, he turned from the white blanketed bush toward a soft yellow light beckoning from within the warm interior of caboose 436788, which stood on the track a few yards away.

Suddenly the soft sounds of nature were broken by the unmistakable wail of a steam locomotive's whistle, followed by the clanging of its bell, then the wheezing and chuffing of it starting up. Quickly, he swung aboard, climbed the steps, and went inside, eager to feel again the rocking and swaying of the old

11

caboose, yearning to hear its life song of "clickety clack, click-ety-clack."

But, alas, his wish must remain unfulfilled, for the "he" is me and caboose 436788 is my studio-home, parked permanently on our family homestead in the Canadian Rockies. It'll never make the main line go clickety-clack again, nor will it rock and sway around curves and up steep mountain grades. Although it is less than a mile, as the crow flies, to the nearest place where trains run, it would take a lot of hard work and money to get it moved back to those tracks. For one thing, cabooses can't fly like crows; for another, they're no longer very welcome in the modern railway scene.

About the whistling and chuffing steam engine? Oh yes, well, one concession I made to the 1980s inside this relic of the 1920s was to hook up a car stereo to a twelve-volt battery. Those taped train sounds sure can seem authentic coming from a pair of loud-speakers! If I were to blow out the lights, turn up the sound, and start swaying from side to side, I could just about make you think we were really moving, even without any real clicks or clacks.

Before you consider me a hopeless train fanatic, let me quickly add that I don't really do this tape and swaying bit more than once or twice a year, and *never* when I'm just in here by myself, honest! Within my drawer full of cassette tape selections there are only about three or four with train sounds. The rest feature flutes by Zamfir and Paul Horn, mellow synthesizers by Kitaro and Andreas Vollenweider; even powwow songs by the Old Agency Drummers of the Blood Indian Reserve. Sometimes, in the middle of winter, I think of the summer Pow-Wow season, so I put on a tape of Indian dance songs, push my chair up against the desk to make more room, then practice a few rounds up and down the narrow aisle. Makes me wonder if any other railroad caboose has ever reverberated to the sounds of war whoops, bells and big rawhide drums.

As for not being a fanatic, any guy whose family owns *four* cabooses has a hard time claiming complete innocence—espe-cially when those four are still on their own wheels, parked on short sections of tracks, as if some old railroad had just abandoned them here years ago.

Our reasons for having them seem simple enough to me. There are four children in our family, three of them teenaged boys. That alone says something to those of you in similar situations. Add to that the limited space in our basic family home, which is a simple frame cabin, small and without separate personal rooms. With the kids always at home—they participate in a correspondence school—you can imagine that our house some-times feels mighty crowded.

Now if Mama and I—or even just one of us—had jobs to go to during the day, that would help a bit. But that's where the final reason for having cabooses comes in: We both work at home as writers and can be pretty temperamental.

Readers of our family's books about natural living and native cultures might expect us to move out into a circle of tepees, instead of refurbishing old trains. We do that at times, especially when the days are long, hot and lazy. But try teaching four kids, baking bread and running a mail-order book business inside a tepee, especially when it turns thirty or forty below zero outside. *Then* you really begin appreciating the idea of roomy, insulated cabooses!

Of course, since our books are history oriented, there's also an inspirational side to having old railroad cars. For instance, the windows I look out from when at my desk have framed the gazes of countless railroad men. Who knows how often lights shone out through these windows and into winter snows, just as in our opening scene? How many steam engines have puffed and whis-tled, pulling an endless variety of trains and cars with this caboose on the back?

Life began in 1922 for my caboose. The "Roaring Twenties" hang unseen in its aisles. Maybe one of the carpenters who helped build its tongue-and-groove interior at Canadian Pacific's Angus Shops in Montreal was a dapper young gent who wore a straw hat in his off-hours and chauffeured his lady around in a long coupe with bulbous headlights.

During the tough times of 1929, there must have been one or two among the older conductors working in here who lost a good part of their savings in the stock market. Then, in the "Dirty Thirties" that followed, some of the young brakemen who stomped their boots on these floors must have been worrying about parents and families "back home on the farm."

In the early forties, hardy men in overalls and woolen coats no doubt swore frequently in here about Hitler and Mussolini, as they warmed their hands by the stove or washed them in the little round sink. Rail traffic was heavy during the war years, so this caboose traveled a lot. Canada's prosperity, afterward, did nothing to slow it down, either. During the 1950s, soot from the stacks of steam engines begin to fall less and less often on the tarred canvas roof that is over my head, as Canadian Pacific switched from steam to diesel power.

Traveling back and forth across the Canadian Rockies, I may have seen this caboose myself, during its final years of work in the 1970s. I've been fond of watching trains all my life, although in those days I seldom paid particular attention to cabooses. Wooden cabooses were gone from most big American railroads by then, though they were still fairly common in Canada. But, I had no idea that I'd be getting one of them, or I would have watched them more closely.

A LITTLE CABOOSE HISTORY

We'll hear the details of how that happened a little later, but first, let's identify what a caboose is. If you're an old sailor, you may prefer this definition given by Webster's: "A deckhouse where the cooking is done; a . . . galley." The kind of caboose we're talking about is generally defined as being, "a car on a freight train, used by the train crew."

"Caboose," "cab," "shack," "crummy," "hack," "buggy," "brain box," "van," "waycar" and many more terms have been used to describe these unique conveyances that have brought up the rear of North American freight trains for well over a century. The majority of these have been painted red and staffed by crews willing to give the public a friendly wave in passing by.

The first caboose is attributed to some unknown conductor who was said to have sawed a hole in the roof of a boxcar and perched himself on top of boxes so he could watch his train ahead. Auburn & Syracuse conductor Nat Williams is among the first on record to use a caboose for train service, having converted a small boxcar back in the 1840s by furnishing it with a wooden box to serve as a seat and an upended barrel to double as an office desk and lunch counter. In addition, he carried sturdy containers for such emergency supplies as tools, chains, lanterns and flags.

By the second half of the nineteenth century, railroads generally followed standard designs in building their cabooses, based on a need for crews to have office space and living quarters. Most had three or four bunk beds with mattresses and storage underneath, a stove and cooking counter, plus writing desk and chairs for the daytime work.

The most notable feature of a standard caboose is its cupola—its "observation tower." Reached by steel ladders, its upstairs seats and windows allowed crewmen to look ahead over their trains. This was valuable back in the era when wheels often heated up, trailing telltale smoke which warned of potential danger if the train was not stopped.

For many decades before the invention of air brakes, men had to go along the tops of trains to turn small, steel wheels which tightened each car's brakes. The caboose gave them shelter in between such work; also when switching was being done along the route, crews used the caboose to rest and warm up. Many serious accidents have been averted over the years by alert crews watching ahead from cabooses on the backs of trains.

But now, steam engines are gone from most railroads, and changing technology has eliminated several major reasons for trains having cabooses. For instance, self-lubricating roller bearings on car wheels generally prevent hotboxes, with their trails of warning smoke. Furthermore, there are trackside computer devices that monitor each passing wheel, conveying the information to train crews instantly. Modern braking systems have removed the need for brakemen to take dangerous walks along the tops of cars; and motel-like crew hostels have replaced the portable cars where trainmen could sleep and cook. Besides, instead of the crews of five or six men per train, as in the past, most are now down to three, and some have only two. All members can now ride together in the engine, up front.

In 1967, the Florida East Coast Railway became the first mainline railroad to operate trains without cabooses. Instead, rear-of-train monitoring was performed by electronic devices. Predictions of an increase in accidents failed to materialize; rather, the line has earned the Harriman Trophy for employee safety numerous times since then.

Railroad companies point out that computer boxes can check the safety of today's long trains while men on cabooses could not see halfway to the front of them. Another important change is that many trains now run only from "point A" to "point B," without stopping partway for switching or other work. Of course, company economists have relished the thought of eliminating the added weight and expense of these hundred-thousand-dollar steel cars, which must be kept maintained and staffed.

Since a book like this cannot stand in the way of progress, we will not go further into the politics of cabooses. I'll certainly be as sorry to see them go as I was to watch the demise of steam engines. At one time, I worked on mainline locomotives as a fireman; now that occupation hardly exists. Yet, I have not lost my interest in railroads because of it.

Of course, there are those who think railroads should be closed down altogether—that they are as outdated as cabooses, steam engines and locomotive firemen. After all, passenger stations are now few, and passenger services are just skeletal remains of the past; the still numerous freight trains have a habit of sometimes derailing and spilling deadly chemicals. Yet, only a fool would advise abandonment of our remaining railway system, when highways are clogged and crumbling, while airlines struggle with air congestion and pollution. This book is certainly meant to encourage further thought on the value of our railroads, with the hope that future transportation schemes will find already-existing rail corridors to have many advantages.

CHAPTER TWO

Across the Rockies in My Own Caboose

But I rode to the county seat in state,
  In the red caboose of the local freight
And I watched the track slip out and away,
  With the telegraph poles, across the plain;
Prairie and track and the moving train.

. . .

. . . Coming in from the dark and wet
  To the shelter and warmth of the rough clean shack
At the end of a freight on the track;
  Never so far that my dream turned loose
Would not carry me back to the old caboose.

—MAUDE K. BACKLUND

It was the summer of 1978 and we were planning ahead for our winter's writing work. I told my wife, Beverly, I'd be compiling a large photo book about railroads, but that I hadn't figured out where to spread out all the material and pages. At that time, there were only three kids in the household (daughter Star came a year later); the family cabin measured about twenty by thirty feet. "Why don't you build yourself a little studio," she suggested helpfully. "Then you can spread out your work just as you like."

About that same time, I happened to hear a friend lamenting about four old, dilapidated cabooses sitting on the outskirts of his city, Calgary. He thought they should be preserved as historical relics rather than simply destroyed for scrap. When I mentioned this to Beverly, she said I should take a look at them to see if one would do for the room that I wanted. We both realized this would make an ideal environment for creating a book about railroads.

On asking around at Canadian Pacific's Alyth railyard in Calgary, I was directed to a dusty, weed-grown siding across the mainline, where discarded railway cars were frequently parked. There, I found five worn and tired old wooden cabooses; all of them had obviously been subjected to the ravages of dust storms, prairie blizzards and vandalism. Their windows were busted, doors unhinged and most fittings of any value stripped and taken. Looking them over, I felt like a kid who had been told he could have his first car, but that he must select it out of a junk yard!

However, as I began to inspect those veterans more closely, I realized that under their scars and wounds remained the sturdy evidence of good wood and expert carpentry. On asking CP Rail's purchasing agent, at his downtown office, I learned that for $600 I could have my pick, taking one "as is, where is," minus the wheels. Their basic bodies certainly couldn't be duplicated at twice the price; even in their shabby condition, the initial cost would be a deal.

Of course, there was the problem of those darned Rocky Mountains, sitting solidly between the old cabooses and our home. That made the idea of hauling one by truck seem very expensive. Could I have one moved on tracks, I inquired, and would this be cheaper? Quick inspection by an authorized employee showed that the one I had in mind was still roadworthy. "She's gone over a million miles already," he said with a wink. "I think she'll manage a couple more hundred." Shipping clerks looked through their books until they found an especially low rate, fifty-nine cents per mile, which applied to the movement of certain private freight cars. Meanwhile, I located another fellow who already had his own caboose, including wheels that he didn't want. I bought them from him at far less than the $1,200 the company thought they were worth, arranging to make a swap after my caboose arrived home.

It was late fall before this caboose purchase was finally settled; there wasn't much time if we were to make the move before winter. Yet, with the passing of each day, my ideas for the project expanded. Most importantly, I didn't want to see the old thing dragged shamefully out of town like an old wreck. Surely there could be some kind of respectable ceremony for an old caboose making its final journey.

THE JOURNEY HOME

The railway's public relations people are always concerned about their corporation's image, so I went to see them. The idea of an illustrated kid's book about "the old red caboose goin' home" struck a chord with Larry Bennett, a young and imaginative member of Canadian Pacific's PR team. He brought me to Superintendent D. G. Stewart, the boss of CP Rail's Alberta South Division, who was *very busy* keeping lots of multimillion dollar trains moving all over his trackage. A $600 caboose would understandably have a hard time entering his thoughts, much less his complex railroad system.

But the sun shone bright on that day, as Mr. Stewart's ear was caught by Larry Bennett, his imagination probably fired by memories of long-ago days, working around cabooses as an ordinary employee. He gave me a letter of introduction that stated my purpose with the caboose, gave me permission to be on it *and* to ride the train that was to bring it home. The letter even asked employees to extend "every possible courtesy" during my time on the project. That was a singular offer of help at just the right moment; I've treasured the results of it ever since.

For the next cold week, my home was the old caboose, after I did some initial cleaning out of the worst trash and garbage. There were empty wine bottles, dirty newspapers, torn rags, broken pieces of furniture and, in one corner, an even more gross (though thoroughly air-dried) pile of evidence that tramps, hoboes and other ne'er-do-wells had shacked around in here. With a mop and many buckets of water (hauled from a nearby slaughterhouse), I washed everything: floors, walls, ceilings, cupola and the insides of three very spacious storage bunks whose tops had served as beds for countless CP Rail trainmen. Those had been hard-working men, doing important jobs that helped support their families and their nation. After liberal doses of soap and disinfectant were used along with the wash water, we got rid of some of the temporary signs of decadence. Then, the fifty-plus years of respectful treatment quickly began to be evident again in this old caboose.

During the second morning of my cleaning work, an icy wind began blowing in the season's first blizzard. Soon, snow came down in almost horizontal torrents, as it often does on the prairie. The wind was blowing so hard that snowflakes entering through the glassless rear window blew clear through the caboose and back out the other end. In between, it was mighty cold and unpleasant for working. The caboose's stove had been taken out long before; all that remained was a hole in the ceiling for the chimney.

The only visitor I had during those clean-up days was a railroad policeman, who came by to see how things were going. Larry Bennett had introduced me to the railroad's chief of police, who in turn informed his men of my work. He had said to me, "It wouldn't do for your story to tell how you got arrested!"

I also got waves and greetings twice a day from a whole bunch of people—passengers riding aboard Canada's premier train, *The Canadian*. One passed in each direction daily on the transcontinental mainline, which ran adjacent to our track. Thus, my old girl rubbed shoulders day in and day out with a world-famous train, even though she herself had fallen into sad decline.

An historic event took place on that main line while we were there. After twenty-five years, *The Canadian* ran for the last time under Canadian Pacific Railway sponsorship. In 1955, this had been CP's international flagship, a drawing card for tourists from all over the world to travel through Canada. Suddenly, its operation was taken over by the Canadian government, in the form of VIA Rail Canada, similar to Amtrak in the United States. The train is now officially VIA Nos. 1 and 2, *The Canadian*. I knew

nothing about this change until the day after, when I happened
to hear about it on the radio. By coincidence, I photographed
that last CP train just as it passed my caboose.

Arrangements had been made for a switch engine to come
over and pick up my caboose on Monday morning, hauling us
to the caboose-shop tracks, where a water hose and other cleaning
materials helped me complete my task. After some further repairs
and inspection, we would leave from there and join a freight train
headed over the Rockies.

No. 8103 was our switcher; I saw it way down the line when
it first started heading toward our weed-grown spur. This maneuver required a crossing of mainline tracks, which in turn took
time and special permission from the dispatcher. Our switch had
to be unlocked, entered, and locked back up to make sure no
mainline train would accidentally follow the switcher in. Im-
proper handling of this procedure has been responsible for many
deadly train accidents, including one near Calgary with passengers, not long after this caboose event.

A flash of these kinds of thoughts went through my mind as
the switcher approached, its headlight bearing down on us. Suddenly I realized that my caboose and I were about to enter the
mainline world of modern railroading, and the thought made my
blood tingle.

The switcher lurched from side to side, flanges on its wheels
loudly squealing in protest as it slowly made its way down our
seldom-used rails. A switchman stood on the front step of the
engine to guide the engineer with hand signals. They did not
know that I was aboard, nor that they were about to become a
small part of my exciting adventure.

The switchman signaled the engineer to a stop just short of
my caboose. Then he got off the engine step and pulled up on
an iron lever at the corner of my caboose, causing the coupler's
knuckle to open. Next, he signaled for the engine to move ahead
slightly, until its coupler joined with ours. He didn't see me at
the window opening as he walked to the other end and pulled a
similar lever which made us uncouple from the four cabooses

behind. (Later, as we pulled away, I wondered what their fate would be. Would there be other men with dreams like mine, coming in time to save them?)

The back door rattled as the switchman pushed and kicked on it to get in. When it finally flew open, he came inside as one would enter an old piece of junk headed for the scrap heap. He gave a start when he saw me heading toward him; I was just going to help open the door.

"What are you trying to do in here?" he asked in a gruff voice, his eyes making a quick inspection. "Trying to go for a little ride?" He must have thought I was either a hobo or a vandal.

Putting on my best smile, I said, "I've just bought this caboose and I'm trying to fix it up a little before I get it home."

The atmosphere changed instantly. At the same time, the switchman noticed my mop and bucket, plus sleeping bag, tools and other stuff. "Oh, you did, eh?" he replied, still trying to get over the surprise. "And now what are you going to do with it?" He still looked pretty puzzled, trying to figure out this young fellow, wearing an engineer's cap and two long braids, standing in the middle of an abandoned caboose, claiming it was his.

But when I told him that my wife and I publish books over in British Columbia, that we wanted to use the caboose as an office and that it might also serve as a schoolhouse for our kids, *then* he had something to understand. He relaxed and took on the friendliness for which railroad workers have always been noted. When I added that I was also working on a photostory of the trip, my status rose even higher. Apologetically, he said, "Jeez, and here I thought you were just some common bum trying to latch a free ride."

Taking a hurried look around the inside, he opened up all the closet doors along his way, half mumbling to himself, "Aw, just checking." I found this "checking" to be a common habit among railroad men visiting my caboose, even long after I moved my things in and got settled. While strangers might ask hesitantly if they could come in or go up into the cupola, old brakemen and conductors march right in and inspect everything. Must be a habit left over from the days when cabooses were regularly assigned to their crews and newcomers were liable to find all sorts of belongings left behind.

By the time this switchman finished his cursory inspection, he was needed outside to line the switch for our move onto the main line and beyond. So far, the old caboose was doing just fine, having completed its first trial run of several dozen yards down that rusty back track. After that, we spent the next half hour or more working our way back and forth through tracks and switches in the Alyth yard, picking up two more cabooses along the way. These were modern ones that had just come in on trains and were now being brought for servicing to the same shop area for which we were bound.

At last we arrived on the caboose-shop tracks, which were filled with yellow-painted, steel-bodied units. However, the railroad did still have a few wooden ones left in local service, and we happened to get parked right next to one of these. At a quick glance, it looked the same as mine, although it was some twenty years newer, having been built during the steel-shortage years of World War II. Still, it was like the meeting of two old friends in the midst of a gathering of busy, mainline "newcomers." Amid that sea of modern, shiny yellow, mine stood out as the only one still wearing the fading remnants of Canadian Pacific red.

A couple of shopmen looked up to see what new work the switch engine had brought for them. Our switchman walked past where they stood and said something, gesturing my way, after which the two came over and climbed the steps to get inside. After exchanging greetings and similar explanations, as before, one of the two said he was the shop foreman and that he had been given instructions to assist my efforts at cleaning up the caboose. Could I write him up a list of broken and missing pieces so he could have his men keep their eyes open for replacement parts that might still be on hand?

Before I could recover from this surprise, he pointed out the water hose, hooked to a large nozzle nearby, and told me to come along so I could get some cleaning gear to make my job more thorough. As a result, I spent the next couple of hours scrubbing out years of dirt, watching streams of black water running across the wooden floor and out the doors at both ends. By the time I finally shut off the flow, there was a dramatic change in appearance. Good layers of brown, green and white paint emerged from under the layers of grease and grime. It had been fifteen or twenty years since the car was last assigned to a regular crew that kept its appearance neat.

When I brought the hose back outside, a shop worker walked up with an armful of old, wood-framed windows he had found leaning against the back of a shed. He took them inside, tried them in my empty window frames and pronounced them suitable. There were enough to close up all the downstairs openings. In addition, he had found several rolls of black canvas, complete with metal rods, that turned out to be well worn but still very serviceable window shades of the kind that are rolled up on a wooden stick and fastened over the top of each window with a leather strap. From then on, my home had privacy whenever I wanted it.

Shortly afterward, another fellow came bearing a tall, square-shaped tin can that looked a bit beaten and dirty. Cleaned up and set into an empty square tray at the back of my "kitchen counter," it became the main water container, its little brass spigot sticking out over the counter's small, round sink. The foreman later brought an almost new insulated metal jug to sit beside the old one, saying it would be more hygienic for drinking water.

Along with the odds and ends I had listed as missing from my caboose, I had also included a few more notable items, such as lamps, stove and mattress. I didn't actually expect to get any of these, but wanted to make the list complete, nevertheless. The foreman showed up after a while and said, "I think we can locate a couple of bad-order lamps to make this place look good, and we can get you a passable mattress, but those old pot-bellied caboose stoves took off out of here like hot pancakes on a cold morning when the company changed the cabooses over to oil heat."

I solved the stove problem later by going downtown and searching through Calgary's second-hand stores until I found a workable little upright coal burner that cost me only forty dollars, although I had a time talking a city bus driver into letting me bring this rusty relic aboard his coach for its trip back to the railroad yard. The foreman quickly got it hooked up, even drilling holes through its legs so we could bolt it to the floor for the ride home. If you've ever ridden aboard a caboose at the back of a long freight, then you know why most everything inside it is tightly fastened down. Unexpected jolts and bounces are frequent.

By evening, the whole caboose looked quite a bit better than it had the day before, although there were still several important repairs I wanted to make before our big journey. With all the day's rushing, for instance, I never did get a chance to locate glass for the upstairs windows. The trip would be miserable and cold without this. The doors still had no latches to hold them closed. Worst of all, I needed a fresh supply of food, not knowing how long we'd be on the road. The railroad's shipping department had said I would be going out on a freight before daylight; I suddenly panicked at the thought. With another day of work, I would have a complete caboose to ride home, instead of only a partly ready one. Besides, I had hoped to take a few pictures of it before leaving the yard, but my camera had spent all day inside its bag.

It was close to midnight before I fully realized that the departure should be postponed. I rushed upstairs, several flights, to the top of the nearby Alyth yard tower, where the yardmaster was sitting by an array of phones and electronic control panels, surrounded by glass windows through which he could see the whole yard. He was boss of the place and, at that time of night, the only person on duty who could change the orders for moving my caboose.

After introducing myself to this busy individual, I explained my situation to him, but I sensed that he wasn't overly interested. When I finished, he looked at me with a stern face then said, "I have no authority to make changes like that in schedules without some kind of permission from the superintendent. You'll have to see him." When I asked how to reach this man, he said, "Call him at eight in the morning, in his office." And at what time of the morning was my caboose scheduled to go out? "At six," he replied, still showing no sign of emotion.

I went back downstairs, feeling glum and rejected. Outside, in the brightly lit shop area, I felt like a stranger. There sat my very own caboose, yet at the moment it was in the control of others whose ideas were not at all like mine. Picture-taking had no place in their system of keeping trains and cars moving. I hurried over to the car, fearing it might even then be picked up and moved away by a switcher while I was not on it. Soon it would be parked forever, far from moving trains and railroad tracks. Oh, how I wanted those final moments of its long, active life to last just a little longer. Why couldn't I get to finish the repair work properly, then relax and take in a few scenes to tell my grandchildren. . . .

Suddenly, I remembered the letter from the superintendent! In a few minutes I was back upstairs in the yardmaster's office with it. He ignored my presence, calling out various orders to train crews, using telephones and a radio, sometimes looking down at moving lights in the vast, half-darkened yards. Finally, there was a pause, so I said, "Excuse me, I have a letter I'd like you to read." He got up from his swivel chair, took a few steps toward me, adjusted his dark-rimmed glasses and grabbed the paper from my hand.

A moment or two later, his expression seemed to relax. Perhaps the pressure of busy night work in the yard was briefly forgotten as he managed to give me a partial smile. Nodding his head, he said, "Yeah, I guess that'll be good enough authority for me to let you lay over," at which I thanked him and hurried back down to my caboose for a night of sorely needed rest.

The sound of steel wheels turning underneath my bed woke me abruptly very early the next morning. Rattling sounds of a moving train rushed me to the back window. Pulling aside the canvas curtain, I expected to see us rolling out of town on the back of a freight train. With relief, I realized we were simply part of a switching maneuver; a yard crew was bringing a new caboose in and taking some others out.

By the time I got dressed and ready for work, more spare parts were arriving. Someone had found enough glass to close up the cupola windows, which cut off the windy drafts. Also, I got enough leather-covered cushions to fill the four upstairs seats, two facing in each direction. The foreman brought a pair of well-worn brass doorknobs, complete with jambs, to replace the ones some scavenger had taken earlier. One of the workers even rigged up a thin, red rope from one end of the caboose ceiling to the other, tied to a red-painted lever on the emergency brake valve. I first saw one of these as a child, on the wooden coach that served my hometown back in the "Old Country." I recall being warned by my parents *never* to pull on one, and remembered what happened one time when somebody did. But, that's another story. . . .

That next evening came very quickly, it seemed, though not before I'd taken my photos and bought fresh groceries. I stored these in the "grub box," a two-door closet lined with tin, underneath the cupola. Its wooden slats used to hold big blocks of ice, although on this occasion, the weather was so cold that I didn't need any.

Word of my venture had made its way around the yard, so that I was kept busy that last night hosting a steady stream of drop-in visitors. They came with questions, humor and advice, most thinking the whole project was a great idea. A few shook their heads in dismay, wondering why I'd want this "worn-out old van," as they called it in railroad lingo. One or two said the company should have given it to me for free and been glad to get rid of it.

One young fellow in greasy overalls and hard hat said, "This old caboose ain't worth the six hundred dollars you paid for it. For that price, you ought to get one of these newer, metal ones!" His companion added, "Yeah, and this guy's the painter, so he can just cover up your caboose number and change it with one of the new ones. Nobody around here will notice the difference. Then, when they come after Number 436788, they'll pick up the new one instead and even bring you home in it!'' Everyone laughed, and somebody added, "That'll be a bargain, since the new ones cost over fifty thousand dollars!''

In the midst of all the traffic, one of the car repairmen put a new set of brake shoes on the wheels and poured oil into the packing inside the wheel's journal boxes. Stencilled notes on the sides of the caboose told workers that it had been in their shops not too long before, so all felt that it was quite roadworthy.

There were still visitors aboard near midnight, when a switch engine came rumbling down our track. A switchman came up with papers in his hand, checking out caboose numbers. He stopped alongside us and said, "Sixty-seven-eighty-eight? Going on train nine-nine-two, right now.'' That was us! The switcher had come to bring us out into the big freight yard—our last stop before actual departure—and hook us to the train. The carmen waved and wished me good luck, as I stood out on the platform while we rolled away.

Eventually, we came to a stop with a bang, way out in a dark section of the yard. Before the switchman left, I got the information that our train would have sixty-five cars—including us —and that its crew was called for three in the morning. That was barely two hours away, so I quickly got out my bedding and lay down for some rest.

I slept fitfully for the next few hours, and when I finally came wide awake, I noticed that we were rolling along at a slow, steady pace. Lifting a side curtain, I looked out the window just in time to see the flashing red lights of a highway crossing passing in the night. According to my trusty pocket watch (left from firing days on the V.P., fifteen years earlier), it was 5:30; a long day was ahead and I was glad for the extra rest I'd had.

Looking through the back door window, I saw another caboose coupled directly behind us, a modern yellow one with an electric light glowing inside. A trainman in overalls was walking toward the stove with a teapot in his hand. It felt strange to be watching him from my dark abode, wondering if he had any idea that I was aboard.

After washing up at the sink, I climbed upstairs and sat down in the cupola to begin my day of caboose riding. I didn't want to miss a single milepost of the trip. We were still within city limits, so our speed was not too fast. Munching on dry cereal, I looked out over the long string of cars wending their way through the darkness ahead. Far up in front I could see the bright glow of our engine's headlight, illuminating the tracks.

The caboose rolled smoothly and quietly, not at all like one would expect from a fifty-six-year-old wooden veteran. The dark stillness made those first miles of our journey seem almost unreal; I had to turn and look at the other caboose to remind myself that we were really part of a working freight train.

The silhouette of another trainman showed in the cupola behind me, although it was still too dark to see any details. I wondered again if the crew knew that I was there, for I did not want to be mistaken for a trespasser or a tramp. Soon they would see me clearly, as a red streak on the eastern horizon announced the impending sunrise.

It was still dark when we passed the first station, at Aldersyde, just a few miles south of Calgary. Wooden semaphore arms at the top of a tall mast went well with the old wooden station, both of them headed for retirement just like my wooden caboose. There were lights on inside the station, though we passed too quickly for me to see anything more. Had I been able to look inside the adjoining freight shed, I would have seen a handsome buggy being built by the resident operator (formerly called the "station agent"), though I didn't learn about that until another visit to the station a few months later.

I did catch a quick glimpse of the operator standing out on the station platform near the track, holding a long, thin stick in one hand. It was a train-order hoop, which he passed to the conductor, who stood down on the steps of his caboose for that purpose. From papers that were fastened to this hoop, he learned what trains we would be meeting on the line ahead, plus any other information pertinent to our safe and efficient journey. Now, as I write these lines, train-order hoops are just a memory; they are gone, along with the Aldersyde station, its operator and his handmade buggy. But for those few brief moments of our passing, they sure made ideal props in this almost fantasy story.

Some miles down the line, we slowly ground to a halt. Up ahead, I could see the glow of an approaching headlight, which meant we were meeting another train. I took this opportunity to go back and visit the "rear-end" part of our crew. The conductor, to whom I showed my letter from the superintendent, said they had been advised by radio that someone was sleeping in the old caboose, although they had thought it was a track worker or some other traveling employee. They invited me to stay back and ride with them, but I explained why my own car was much preferred.

Sunrise was well under way by the time our freight train started up again. We were now headed southeast across the open prairie. Looking out at a seemingly endless expanse of land and a vast blue sky, with notebook and pencil in hand and my camera at my side, I tried to record this final journey of my retiring caboose. The following excerpts are from those notes:

Boy, I'm sure surprised at how well this caboose rides—I expected to be tossed and turned; I expected dust to fly and things to fall, or even break. But so far, it's just been a smooth ride. And here the fellows at the caboose shops had told me I'd better ride in back with the crew because their newer caboose would have a modern "cushion ride." I told them, "Heck, can you imagine me telling my grandkids someday that I could have ridden this old caboose across the Rockies on its last run but decided to take a "cushion ride" instead? No way!"

. . . We've just passed over a *big* long bridge near Carmangay. I had planned to stand out on the edge of my steps and get a dramatic photo looking way down. . . . But we were really rolling along; when I stepped outside and took one look down, I decided a photo from up in the cupola would do just fine!

Looking to the front, I see that we have not one, but four locomotives—big red ones with white stripes. No wonder we're traveling at such a lively pace, especially since the track is virtually level and there are few curves. It's hard for me to judge the speed, since there are few reference points out here on this prairie. I was warned to expect quite a jolt each time the train started up or slowed down, caused by the slack running out of sixty-five pairs of couplers. But just like the "cushion ride" business, there's not much to this slack problem. I wonder if those shopmen ever ride on the cabooses they fix.

Just passed Nobleford, a little prairie ranching community with a nice, old station [since removed]. An old man and a black hunting dog stood in the early morning shade of a tall grain elevator near the station, watching us go by. The old man waved, and I saw that he had a shotgun across his back, along with a belt full of shot shells. These vast grain fields support lots of plump pheasants; I suspect the old gentleman is planning to have bird-under-glass, or at least a plain old pheasant stew. The government brought these birds from Europe and introduced them on the prairies many years ago—maybe to replace the buffalo they so thoughtlessly allowed to be exterminated.

. . . I'm back after a lengthy stop at Coalhurst, an important junction. There was no time to write, as I was outside taking photographs. Who would have thought they'd pose this old caboose coupled directly to four big engines? Actually, I couldn't have arranged a scene like that if I'd tried; it just happened to be part of the switching maneuvers.

At the Coalhurst yard limits, the conductor came up and uncoupled us from the rest of the train, tightening the hand brakes to keep the strong gusts of wind from blowing us down the line. The engines then moved our train over to another track before they came back to pick us up, this time leaving the yellow caboose behind. "Your vehicle's got good brakes," said the conductor, as he released the steel brake-wheel out on the platform.

"Stem-winders," they call these kinds of brakes on which the wheel is at the top of a long iron rod. Old-time boxcars had them sticking above their roof lines. In those days, brakemen walked over the tops of their trains, tightening the wheels with the aid of wooden clubs. After my attempt to stand out on the steps while going over that bridge, I can only marvel with awe and respect at those tough old-timers. Imagine, walking along the snow covered tops of rocking and swaying freight cars during a winter blizzard, at night. One slip and it was over the side; maybe *way* over, if the train was just heading up a canyon or some other rugged place.

At one point, the conductor said the engines had more switching to do and that I should go ride in them for a while. When I agreed, he called the engineer on his portable radio and said, "One of your brothers from L.A. is coming up to catch a ride with you." That was a reference to my time as a locomotive fireman for the Union Pacific Railroad, out of Los Angeles, after I graduated from high school. Like others of the trade, I had belonged to the Brotherhood of Locomotive Firemen and Enginemen.

But when I stepped up into the engine cab at Coalhurst, the man at the controls took one look at me and my braids and evidently decided the conductor was playing a joke on him. Only after I explained myself and showed him the superintendent's letter of introduction did he make me feel welcome.

This man spoke with a strong European accent, which is something I had never encountered among Union Pacific engineers. But on this trip, with CP Rail, it seems as though every other employee I've met is from some foreign country; maybe this line should be called the CP International. Yet, they all seem to laugh and joke and get along with each other just the same.

When we finally pulled up to Coalhurst's old clapboard station, I tried to find out what was next on the schedule, but everybody just wanted to look into my caboose and chat. Had a hard time getting away long enough to take a picture. . . . Another old station that won't be in existence much longer. Near it stood several large trees, planted around 1910, when the place was new.

"We're rolling westward now, finally headed for the Rockies. Can't quite see them yet, mainly because of all the dust blown up by this windstorm. The new train crew checked out my caboose before we left the Coalhurst station. "When we get rolling, drop on back to our caboose for some coffee or something," one of them said.

. . . Now, traveling across the favorite hunting territory of my adopted Blackfoot people. Ancestors of my children followed herds of buffalo through here, setting up their tepees in sheltered places.

We just passed a spot they used to call "Left Bank," along the Old Man River. Beverly's "grandpa" Willie Eagle Plume once told me how the mean warrior Calf Shirt was killed there by traders whom he was harassing. He was so ornery and tough that they first poisoned, then shot him, finally stuffing him down a hole chopped into the frozen river before he would die. . . .

Just made my visit to the back for that cup of tea and conversation (climbing *very* carefully over the couplers in the open space between my back porch and theirs!). Boy, the conductor sure changed the relaxed mood of this trip for me! When I asked him what's in those long, white tank cars up ahead, he laughed, looked over at his brakeman, then told me very seriously, "Propane! If anything happens to even just one of them, there won't be enough left of you *or* your caboose for your wife to pick up and carry home!" He did mention that the car *directly* in front of me is empty, as required by law, but added that, if anything went wrong, that single car "won't make a damned bit of difference." Gee, thanks for the travel tip. . . .

Leaving Fort Macleod, I can finally see the mountains, although the wind is still blowing. Over on the highway, paralleling our tracks, I also see a familiar-looking red truck. The whole family has shown up to accompany us in the truck for the next few miles. During our stop at the fort, they all came inside briefly, and when it was time to go, none of the kids wanted to get off. "It's your caboose, isn't it, Papa?" they wanted to know. I swallowed hard, especially when two of them started getting tears in their eyes. Conductor Ernie Shire solved my problem by stating in a very firm voice, "You have no authority to take anyone else aboard. Besides, it would be very dangerous." When I told them about exploding propane cars, they suddenly lost their enthusiasm and willingly got back off.

Ernie Shire just left, after riding with me in this cupola for a while. He said, "I practically lived in one of these for thirty years. We just gave up our last wooden one about two years ago—an old-timer, built in 1913. [Son Okan has become owner of it since these notes were made.] We had it regularly on this same run up to Crowsnest; it was just like a second home. I've brought many a shovelful of coal to fill that bunk; also our own ice, and coal oil for the lamps. I used to have the run from Lethbridge to Medicine

Hat and we'd be gone from home all week, eating and sleeping in our 'crummy.' Sometimes we'd get the same caboose for four or five years, so we'd fix them up real nice inside."

At last, we're right up in the Rocky Mountains, ready to pull out of the summit station called Crowsnest. Curves and grades make for a much rougher ride than flat prairies. *Now* I feel the slack running out from between the many cars, and it's getting tough to write. It's more fun to watch the lakes, rivers and waterfalls that we keep winding past.

Had a lengthy layover at Crowsnest, during which our crew was changed and the sun went down while the family came inside for a visit. The kids were all thirsty, so I gave them canned spring water from my grub box, provided from company larders. Since Shane prefers pop over water, I told him, "Here, have some CP Rail pop." Boy, you should have seen him eagerly peeling the little metal tab back for a refreshing drink. He was almost done with it before somebody let him in on the joke.

The new conductor is a friendly fellow named "Red" Donovan, who added to the trip's excitement by saying, "So, you got the old 6788. I worked for years on that caboose; must have ridden half a million miles on it!" The historian in me loves to hear that kind of talk; sure adds to my appreciation of this rolling relic.

"This is just like old-home week," he said. "You're just bringing this old caboose home, that's all you're doing." Turns out it was stationed in Cranbrook as far back as "Red" can remember, working right up the valley where we live, calling the Rockies its home. "Let me think, here," he said, scratching his abundant red locks. "It belonged to Rollie Cox back in forty-eight and forty-nine [meaning it was assigned to Conductor Cox and his crew], then it went to "Black Jack" Sutherlin. He had it for quite a while; I worked with him on it quite a lot in the fifties, when we still had steam engines. I think old "Black Jack" was about the last one that owned it on the main line. After that, it was assigned to the wayfreights, running up to Kimberley and Skookumchuck, out near where you live. It was still around in the early part of the seventies, but I don't know when it finally left. For a while, we were losing our old cabooses at the rate of about one a week, replaced by those modern things that stay with the trains and travel all over."

I asked the conductor if cabooses were like steam engines, in that crews like some much better than others. "Oh, hell yes," he replied emphatically. "Some of them rode so darned rough you couldn't stand them, while others rode like Cadillacs. That one you got was about as good as any of them; I always liked it. When they put in the plywood paneling—nailed it right over the old V-joint boards—they made them about fifty percent warmer in the winter-time. Before that, we had to put up with a lot of drafts; always had to keep them old pot-bellied stoves going near full blast."

We're stopped at Fernie for a meet with another train. There's light coming in here from the town, outside, so I'll take the opportunity to write a few more lines. Talk about a fantastic ride! Sitting alone, up in the cupola, warmth floating up from a fire in the stove down below. It's pitch-black outside as we roll over heavy steel rails winding their way along unpopulated stretches of mountains and rivers. In the darkness, all the rattling and clattering makes it seem that we're doing a hundred miles an hour, or more, though I'm sure our speed is not even half that fast.

I try not to think what would happen if this old caboose suddenly decided its last mile had come, especially along some of these mountain ledges. Often, I can't even see the lights of our lead engine making its way around several curves ahead. Don't think I'd come out too well, up here in this wooden box—not even a seat belt to hold me in place—if we started to fall. . . .

Next day: It's 7:15 in the morning; we're headed out of Cran-brook's freight yard. I've come in and out of this town many times. [We do our family shopping here.] But I never imagined to see it fading into the distance from up in the cupola of my own caboose!

Only two diesels are up on the front of this train, a "local" known as the "Skookumchuck wayfreight." It makes a daily hundred-mile round trip up our valley, switching at various sidings, including one at a big pulp mill, on the way. We're hauling empty flat cars, to be refilled with logs, plus hoppers full of wood chips that may become the paper for a book you will read.

Of special interest is the caboose behind us, the *last* regularly assigned wooden one in the whole region. Although painted the newer yellow, it makes a fitting partner for my red one's final run. Its boss, Conductor Ferg, is sitting at his desk doing the train's paperwork by the light of a lantern, while the proverbial teapot sits on a stove nearby. When I introduced myself, a few minutes ago, he said his train orders had included a note about my presence aboard here. . . .

My notes ended about there, although the trip didn't. At Skookumchuck, we got left in the siding next to a tiny train-order station, waiting for a different wayfreight to take us one stop further north. The twenty-mile stretch of track between Skookumchuck and that next place, Canal Flats, goes along my favorite piece of river-bottom wilderness, right past where we live. For that reason, it was of special significance.

By the time that final wayfreight train showed up, the family had found my side-track location and joined me for another visit. The new conductor shall remain nameless because he looked the other way as we took off, while our little boys sat very quietly with me upstairs in the cupola. Though the ride was uneventful and lasted less than an hour, it was one they will no doubt always remember.

Actually, the biggest adventure involving this lengthy caboose journey was yet to come, although our trip by rail was now over. Managers of the lumber mill on whose siding we finally came to rest allowed me to set up one last photo in their yard. It featured my caboose at the back of two loaded log cars, "hauled" by their own vintage diesel switcher, which was also a CP Rail "pensioner" that they had bought secondhand.

The most common question asked by friends and visitors to our home has been, "How did you get your caboose way down here?" referring to our somewhat remote wilderness homestead. When I'm in a lighthearted mood, I reply, "We floated the thing across the river from the mainline tracks," although that would have been impossible, since there is a roadless piece of dense brush and a backwater channel in between.

Actually, I had made arrangements for a local trucking firm to do the hauling and for a heavy-duty crane to come and lift the car on and off its tracks. The crane's owner was an enterprising Hungarian refugee named Frank Sandor, who wanted to save me money by loaning me a gooseneck trailer on which I should carry the caboose behind our family truck! Perhaps I didn't explain the car well enough and he was picturing one of those little four wheeled bobbers that European trains used to haul around, instead of a thirty-foot vehicle weighing fifteen tons. I was glad I turned down the offer after I saw the caboose's impact on Henderson's heavy-duty truck and low-boy trailer. My own truck would have probably sunk several inches, right down into the ground!

In fact, even the crane was not quite up to the task at hand; it could barely raise one end of the caboose, never mind trying to lift the whole thing very far into the air. Lumber mill personnel came to our rescue with a gigantic machine made for lifting truckloads of fresh logs. With two of its huge, jawlike grips placed firmly under the body, it lifted my caboose easily, allowing the many-wheeled trailer to back underneath the car before it was lowered back down.

Secured with heavy cables, our peculiar load rolled out onto the highway, bringing comments from passing truckers over their C.B.s, one of them warning our truck driver, "Watch out with that big camper you're hauling." Leading the way in our own truck, we traveled a few miles over highway pavement before turning off onto a rutted dirt road that winds its way downhill toward our home.

The poor truck driver hadn't seen this part of the route, or he might have turned the job down. The ruts were bad, the curves narrow, and a forest of trees crowded our passage from both sides. The final few hundred yards involved a bumpy hill so steep that our own truck requires four-wheel drive to get up in all but good weather. It was too late for the driver to back out, or he would surely have done so. As it was, we all held our breaths, wondering if we might just end up with a big pile of firewood, should the caboose break loose and careen down that hill on its own.

Safe arrival at the bottom did not mean our troubles were over, however. There was still the problem of a much-too-weak crane, which could not lift the caboose clear of its trailer, underneath. We figured to solve this by raising only one end at a time, blocking that up with beams, then raising the other end.

The idea was feasible, all right, but several factors made it unusually difficult.

For one thing, neither truck driver nor crane operator was officially required to perform such work as unloading and blocking; that required members of another union who were not at hand. I might have done much of the job myself, except that I had accidentally slipped and fallen in the wet darkness of the previous night, tearing ligaments in one knee that left me limping around in deep pain, using a cane for support. The crane operator was not much better off, having recently had surgery on a cracked kneecap or something. To top these problems off, we were running so far behind schedule that it was getting dark, while at the same time big snowflakes came swirling down to announce the start of the season's first blizzard in our valley.

There's nothing much worse than to be stymied during a complicated moving operation while expensive equipment sits idle, running up tremendous charges by the hour. The fifteen-mile trip from lumber mill to home was already more expensive than the whole trans-mountain journey of over 250 miles, and I still didn't have my caboose unloaded and settled down!

I'll spare you the further details of these woes, except to say that those two fellows wanted to get out of that storm and back home. However, I didn't volunteer to drive them back in our truck and let them abandon the job until another time. Instead, we all pitched in together, working feverishly by truck headlights, which were bisected by the driving torrents of snow. Although we'd been unable to set the caboose down on its own wheels for a final rest, as I had hoped, I was still very much relieved when the two big units finally rumbled away, spinning their big wheels and throwing gravel at each other as they fought their way back uphill. Several seasons passed before I was able to hire a stronger crane to come down and lift the caboose from its wooden blocking, then set it down firmly on wheels and tracks, where it belonged.

This story wouldn't be complete without the following footnote: Among the friends who soon came to see my caboose was

Allen McKenzie, who asked if any more like it were available. When I mentioned the others, still left behind on the weed-grown Calgary siding, he made arrangements to buy them all, figuring to use them as part of an investment. Having no land of his own, he asked if I'd be willing to store all four here, in return for keeping one of them permanently. Swallowing hard, I told him this would first have to be discussed with my wife.

Since my purpose in settling my family way out here, in the first place, was to live "simply and in harmony with nature," I figured Beverly would frown on any further attempts to bring such symbols of industrial technology into our lives. Thus, I was quite surprised when she said, "Sure, I'll take the other caboose as my own, so I can have a place of privacy as well." In the end, only two of the remaining cabooses came down here, with us paying for the second one and giving it to Okan, whose enthusiasm for trains has become the strongest among our children. However, when an unrelated caboose came up for sale at about that same time, my mother paid for it and gave it to the other kids to use as a playhouse, or whatever they wished. Since then, boxcars have also joined the fleet, among other railway relics. Slowly, this collection is becoming known as the private "Rocky Mountain Freight Train Museum," housing our incorporated Good Medicine Cultural Foundation and Historical Society. Those of you thinking to get your own cabooses, be forewarned about the grand schemes you might end up with!

Above, where it all started out for me—on a prairie siding at the edge of Calgary, Alberta, among a string of derelict cabooses. My No. 436788 is the nearest one, which meant it was taken out of working service last. At the time of this photo I'd already spent some time working on it—replacing shattered windows and broken doors—when the season's first snowfall *blew* in. Canadian Pacific's transcontinental main line, in the center, connects Vancouver with Toronto and Montreal. The second caboose in this line eventually became wife Beverly's; and the fourth now belongs to our son Okan. *Below,* the view from my caboose's cupola, winding our way along the shores of Crowsnest Lake, near the summit of Crowsnest Pass, in the Canadian Rockies. (The large white tank cars up ahead carried the highly explosive propane gas!) AHW PHOTOS

Above, my caboose, on the last leg of its journey across the Rockies to our family home. Here we are near Fort Steele, British Columbia, waiting for the approaching way freight that will take us to our destination, some miles farther up the adjacent Kootenay River. The caboose behind mine, yellow-painted No. 437046, is a comparative newcomer built during World War II. It was the last wooden caboose assigned to mainline service in our area, making this an instant historic scene. *Below,* as an exclamation mark to "final run" across the Rockies, Crestbrook Forest Industries assigned its little mill switcher to pull my caboose a short distance at the back of a real "log train." Beverly and the kids rode up in the cupola, while I took photos. This was the end of its journey by rail.   AHW PHOTOS

The most common question asked about our cabooses is: "How did you get them down to your place?" Fifteen tons is not *that* big of a load for Henderson's heavy-duty trucks, nor for Frank Sandor's four-axle crane. Fortunately, we're out in open country; caboose moving becomes much more complicated if you have to go through towns, under wires, and into tight locations. More than a few caboose owners have given up in the face of sometimes insurmountable moving challenges. *Below,* Okan's caboose, CPR 436504, built in 1913, is settled down to its permanent retirement location after nearly seventy years of rolling across Canada. Ahead of it is the "kids' caboose," bought for them as a present by their grandparents.   AHW PHOTOS

CANADIAN PACIFIC CORPORATE ARCHIVES PHOTO

Real caboose life on the Canadian Pacific, back in the days of steam. The conductor and brakeman are fixing up a "meal on the go," while tagging along behind a way freight in Ontario. *Below,* stepping just beyond the brakeman in the upper photo and then turning around will give you *this* view, if you're aboard *my* caboose. I work at the conductor's traditional place, though my desk is more imposing than his would have been. Sons Okan and Iniskim are working on their HO narrow-gauge scale model project called the "Kootenay River Scenic Railway." It's part of their home schooling ("shop class," among other titles), but they're also earning some money by helping me photograph and write a series of magazine articles based on it.

BRIAN CLARKSON, CRANBROOK PHOTO

Left, our cabooses were quite spartan when brand new, some sixty, seventy-five years ago. Here is CPR No. 436804, part of a fleet built in the summer and fall of 1922. My caboose was in that fleet, built just sixteen ahead of this one. Ten years of residence by our family has wrought many additions. The conductor's desk is at the left, his wide bunk behind that. Two long benches on the right fold down to make part-time beds for the two brakemen. The floors are hardwood, painted reddish-brown; the ceiling is pine, painted white. An empty notebook with stories, dates, and details to be filled in by countless railroading men—has anyone saved No. 436804?

CANADIAN PACIFIC CORPORATE ARCHIVES PHOTO

Below, the interior of Beverly's caboose, former CPR 436731, built in 1918, has been cleared to make a "shipping department" for our Good Medicine Books, though she has kept the upstairs cupola as her private domain by closing it off with plywood; entry is through a trap door. With the original seats removed and replaced by soft cushions on the new plywood floor, this upstairs cubicle makes a nice sun-room for reading or sleeping.

BRIAN CLARKSON, CRANBROOK PHOTO

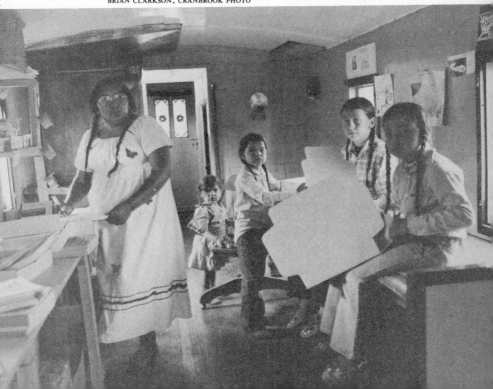

PHOTO BY HENRY R. GRIFFITHS, JR.

Above, a yellow-painted steel caboose trails two hardworking 2-8-8-0's pushing on the rear of this seventy-two-car Union Pacific freight train, photographed in October 1953. The train's lead engine smokes far up ahead on the autumn prairie. Scenes like this were still fresh memories for most UP enginemen when I hired on as fireman nine years later. *Below,* winter on the Branchline: A yellow-painted UP wooden caboose waits while the crew does a bit of switching. The rear brakeman is guiding the engineer on this back-up move, while the head brakeman rides on the engine's footboard. The conductor is no doubt at his desk, doing the paper work, tending a pot of coffee.

ROCKY MOUNTAIN RAILROAD PHOTOS

Above, the threat of a fate like this kept crews of wooden cabooses constantly on their toes, especially when traveling at speed. In this 1907 scene in the Northern Pacific yard at Forsyth, Montana, caboose 1267 has been telescoped by a flat car sent rolling down the wrong track by a night switchman. Amazingly, the three crewmen sleeping in this caboose crawled out of the wreckage uninjured! *Below,* steel cabooses tend to survive wrecks in much better condition, as seen by Northern Pacific 1006, being untangled from a rear-end collision between a yard switcher with cabooses and a mainline freight, Missoula, Montana, 1955.

PHOTO BY R. V. NIXON

Above, Northern Pacific caboose 1541 at the rear of NP Extra Freight 1818 east, leaving Polson, in Montana's beautiful Mission Valley, on a spring day in 1946. This car has several unique features, including its bay windows, "fishbellly" bottom and the metal plates instead of marker lamps. NP used bay-window cabooses only for a short time. Notes the photographer: "It was my niece's first train ride. Think she was about five." All aboard! *Below,* the earliest cabooses were often boxcars with doors and windows, including someplace for the conductor to look ahead at his train. Northern Pacific 1705 was photographed with engine 1413 at Staples, Minnesota, around the turn of the century.

CHAPTER THREE

My Grandpa Had One, Too!

When first I kissed my Nancy
    'Twas on a railway train.
A little tuft of thistledown
Danced by the window pane.
She asked me what it symbolized;
    I kissed her to explain.

When first I kissed my Nancy
    'Twas on a railway train.
Her heart was light as thistledown,
Her mouth was soft as rain.
And something weakened in her eyes
    That long asleep had lain.

It seems but yesterday somehow.
Where's thistledown, where's Nancy now?

        —J. CONNELLY

Anton Braun was his name, a tall, robust man with a handlebar mustache, foreman of a roundhouse and its engines for the Hungarian State Railways. My mother was one of his many children—several girls plus a boy. The family worked hard; on the side, Grandpa Anton and my grandma had a little farm and an apple orchard, whose business Grandma, mainly, looked after along with the kids.

When Grandpa Anton came home, after a busy day at the roundhouse, what he liked most of all was to go out and relax in his own private little studio. Like father, like son, they say? How about grandfather and grandson? He had a railroad car for his studio, too!

Of course, my grandpa's car was a little more unique than

this caboose (not that I'm complaining at all). There are quite a few of these cabooses in existence; lots of people own them privately. But hardly anybody had his own railroad car in Hungary, back in the early 1900s. In addition, Grandpa's wasn't just an ordinary freight caboose, like mine; it was a little four-wheeled carriage that had spent its life actually hauling people! From descriptions I've heard, it must have been a little jewel, built sometime in the late nineteenth century, with fancy trim and ornate ironwork.

Relatives have said that I must have gotten my enthusiasm for trains from Grandpa Anton, and no doubt this is true, although there were some railroad employees on my father's Swiss side of the family, as well. But a further point that Grandpa Anton and I have in common is the notion that one car might as well lead to another, although he was satisfied with owning ''just'' two.

His second car was said to have been a larger coach, of more recent vintage (mind you, this was about 1920). Everyone was allowed to go into that one; the whole family used it as sort of a patio and guest house. But the small one was his alone— Grandpa's ''Castle''—and none but the invited dared to go in.

It's too bad I never got to meet Grandpa Anton; I'm sure he and I would have had a lot more in common (though not his appearance as roundhouse foreman!). My mother was long gone from her parents' home by the time I was born. There was a war underway and, afterward, my grandparents were left behind the Iron Curtain. I never did get to meet them.

I don't know what became of Grandpa's little coach, though I like to imagine it still sitting underneath a bunch of old apple trees. The Russians confiscated the farm after the war, and by the time they gave it back, everything was gone or destroyed, including the two cars. The old folks died a few years afterward. Maybe some Russian general had the little coach put on the back of an army truck and hauled to his Baltic vacation spot.

My first thoughts of owning a caboose actually came about fifteen years before I got this one, when I was still in a much different living situation. I was a bachelor, going to school to obtain various degrees. I thought I would become a lawyer or a teacher in some small town along the Pacific Coast. Wilderness life in the Canadian Rockies as an author was not at all in my expectations, especially not with a bunch of kids and relatives helping to carry on very ancient tribal ways.

Old and unusual trains had captured my imagination even back in those school days, after a friend's grandfather began giving me his old issues of *Railroad Magazine*. During summer vacations, I traveled up and down the West Coast in search of interesting trains, especially those pulled by steam, photographing and recording the ones that I found. One result of this peculiar pastime was my first hardbound book, *Rails in the Mother Lode*, which was illustrated with numerous photos of scenes with picturesque trains in California's gold-rush country.

The West Side Lumber Company's little antique narrow-gauge logging line was among those featured in that book. Several photos showed what must have been the cutest and tiniest caboose fleet in the country. Two of the cabooses reminded me of pregnant VWs, while the rest were rather longer and skinnier. In the world of transportation relics, they were real treasures at that time, in the early 1960s.

Trucks replaced this operating rail museum even before my book came out. All the old train equipment was put up for sale. Thus, when I next visited the forlorn little cabooses and heard they could be had for $150 apiece, I determined to buy one of them with funds from the yet-to-be published book. I figured to become the only California college student with his own vest pocket caboose.

But the idea fell through when I couldn't figure out where to put the darned thing. Sure, it was small, but with steel wheels, couplers and other parts, it still tipped the scales at more than two tons. You can't store a thing like that in a college bachelor pad! Besides, it turned out the publisher was only using books as a tax write-off for another business, so he didn't print enough to even cover costs, much less to pay me a royalty. As a student I didn't have the $150 to spare for an old thing like that. Now, I could kick myself for the missed opportunity.

After that experience, I admired others who had better luck getting their own railroad cars, but I didn't expect to try again, myself. How many of those others there are, I couldn't say. I've never heard of a rail car owners' poll. But I can safely say there are "many thousands" of old railroad cars in private hands across North America today, maybe tens of thousands, if you count all the boxcars used for grain storage and chicken coops, plus the flatcars used for rural bridges.

There have been attempts to organize private owners of cabooses into some kind of action group, whether to lobby the government for favorable legislation or simply to share know-how and lore, I don't know. There are very successful organizations for private owners of passenger cars, as well as for operators of small tourist railroads, but the private caboose fraternity prefers to remain uncounted and largely anonymous.

If this vague society were looked at in terms of class, surely the elite among them would be retired conductors and brakemen who took their working cabooses home with them when they left their railroads. The old *Railroad Magazine* frequently had letters from one or another of them. For instance, one old conductor wrote and said the caboose in his front yard stood as a monument to the foot he lost under its wheels one night. We know of a fellow down in Montana who got an old Great Northern caboose from the company as part of a court settlement after he had a similar accident while working in a switchyard.

You can just imagine that some of those old-time railroaders got to liking their cabooses as well as their own homes, after spending years on them. Curtains, rugs, photos and fancy dishes were frequently used to enrich caboose atmosphere by men who lived on them a lot. Incidentally, the holder of probably the longest single caboose assignment on record was Conductor J. O. Pore, who used Nickel Plate Railroad No. 137 continuously from 1914 until his retirement in 1950!

A more dramatic—and sad—example of the close ties that developed between some trainmen and their cabooses is the story of Frank McConnell, a conductor for the Southern Pacific in California. For many years, old Frank was assigned to caboose No. 117, which had nearly as much age as he. He fixed up its interior to look just like a little home; the two were inseparable companions. Eventually, the company said the caboose was getting too old for daily service and would have to be replaced by a new one. The conductor pleaded so long and hard that company officials finally agreed to let him finish out his last few seasons with it.

Then came the day of Conductor McConnell's retirement, at which time the caboose was taken out of service and prepared for scrapping. McConnell went down to the yard to see it every day. Finally, workmen began to tear it apart while he stood by, heartbroken, and watched. Quietly, he went inside once more, closing the door behind him. Suddenly, workmen heard a gunshot and rushed in, only to find McConnell dying in a pool of blood.

THE LADY AND THE CABOOSE

Francene Adelman is at quite the opposite end of the line of those who admire old cabooses. She never worked or even rode on one, but she feels very attached to her own, which sits hidden among the Pembina Hills of Manitoba, far from tracks or even its own wheels. She bought it a few years ago from the Canadian National Railway for $385.

Sleeping up in the cupola is this young lady's greatest delight. She took the seats out from the cupola and put in an open floor (much as Beverly has done with hers), ending up with a cozy upstairs observation room. To help disguise the lack of wheels, she built a wooden porch alongside, in the style of a warehouse dock. At one end, she also added a small enclosed porch, which provides extra storage space. As a result, this elementary school teacher was able to produce her own snug and unique home for less than two thousand dollars, she says.

Caboose ads are regularly seen on the pages of *Trains Magazine*, which serves upward of 100,000 rail enthusiasts. "Train Caboose of Your Own," says one ad, telling you to send $4.95 to a place called "Caboose Retreat," in Indiana, for a pamphlet explaining how.

"You can own this narrow gauge caboose," says another ad, with a photo showing a cute little thing that would be the hit of neighborhood kids (and probably their parents). Five bucks will get you an illustrated brochure about this one from "Classic Caboose," in Coon Valley, Wisconsin. "The ideal attention getter for businesses, restaurants, motels, shops, etc. . . . Could be used for a shop by itself."

A New York outfit called Fantasia Trains offers you all kinds of railroad cars, including cabooses. They serve as brokers between railroads and private buyers, presumably charging a hefty fee, but also taking care of the buying, storing and moving headaches. On some mainline railroads these can be quite severe; don't let the story of my idyllic ride across the Rockies give you false hopes! Fifteen or twenty tons is never an easy load to handle!

CABOOSE CHURCHMEN

Down in North Carolina, the Southern Railroad donated one of its cabooses some years ago as a retirement gift to Bishop Herbert Spaugh, pastor of the Moravian Episcopal Church, who was also quite a railfan. The bishop put his car on a solid foundation, out on his country land, where he used it for "meditation and writing." The interior was rebuilt to suit his own needs, which included electric heating, air conditioning and spacious beds, plus modern cooking and plumbing facilities. Much of the work was done by the new owner, including a finish of knotty-pine paneling.

After a visit to the bishop's caboose, Frank Worthington, retired vice president of the Southern Railroad, offered this recollection: "My wife and I spent a memorable moonlit evening in that caboose. The marker lights were shining brightly and the bishop was dressed for the occasion in an overall jacket, railroader's peaked cap and red bandanna!"

A retired passenger car has a much different kind of atmosphere and personality than a freight train caboose. It is usually quite a bit larger, providing more living space, but it also has more weight and bulk—a liability during moving. About the time that steam engines were disappearing, the last classic passenger cars also left railroad working life. Some were saved by museum groups, tourist railroads and private buyers, but many more were scrapped. Today, most coaches are sold on the private market, where dollar prices usually begin in the thousands and go up.

When Rev. Calvin J. Graves retired from the pulpit in 1935, he decided to fulfill a lifelong wish by obtaining his own railroad car. He planned to make his car into a complete retirement home for himself and his wife, so it had to be something a little more substantial than, let's say, my once derelict caboose. In those days, there were *much* more prestigious pieces of classic railway equipment available, especially for a person like the popular retiring minister!

Yes, the minister definitely outdid the bishop when it came to rolling stock. The Milwaukee Railroad's purchasing agent came up with a real beauty—an old-time heavyweight parlor car of the 1890s. Hand built of mahogany and other fine woods, the car's interior was brightened up by light entering through large, wide windows, while its arched ceilings added a special touch of glamour. The car came fresh off the line, with a bill of sale that included, "all fixtures and furnishings," which would have been pretty elegant in a car of this vintage, back then.

The reverend and his elderly brother-in-law turned carpenters, after the car was moved to a large, grassy suburban lot and set up on a concrete foundation. They added a screened-in front porch, plus a basement containing hot-water heater, fuel room, laundry, workshop and a "well furnished summer den." The area around the car was landscaped with "numerous flowers and shrubs," a berry garden, plus flagstone walkways.

The railroad car/house, itself, consisted of a spacious living room, a combined sleeping room and study, plus bathroom, dinette and kitchenette. The place was equipped with all the modern conveniences of the 1930s.

Collecting train photos and old railroad lore was a favorite pastime with the Reverend Graves. For visitors to his train-car home, he enjoyed recalling a true adventure he himself had taken part in as a teenage boy, back in the 1880s.

At that time, young Graves had a good friend in engineer "Billy" Reese, who ran engine No. 67 on the Utica & Black River Railroad, near the Graves home, back East. Sometimes Billy gave his young railfan friend a ride up in the engine cab.

Such was the case on a certain Sunday morning, when Graves accepted a ride on the engine with Billy instead of going to church as his parents had told him to do. It was only a thirty-five mile run, taking a string of old boxcars from his hometown of Boonville to nearby Utica, New York.

About midway on this trip, the engineer found the train getting out of his control, heading downgrade. Half the old cars had the kind of brakes that require a brakeman to come along and tighten a steel wheel, while the rest had no working brakes at all. These cars were headed for repairs in the shops at Utica. Said Graves of the incident:

"Approaching Marcy Station, six miles from Utica, he blew the runaway signal—several frantic whistle blasts—and, as I learned later, the Marcy operator wired a warning to Utica. When we came in sight of the Utica yards, Billy Reese left his seat, took me by the arm and led me out to the gangway, yelling in my ear: 'When I push, you jump for your life, and I'm behind you!' Evidently he had expected the old gal to jump the rails when she hit the reverse curves. The sixty-seven did rock like a cradle, but she held the rails and at length came to a stop, just as the caboose and the last five box cars toppled over! It was a close shave!"

Young Graves must have been a determined fellow. After the engineer bought him lunch, the two rode back to Boonville together in the same engine cab. He said he made it back in time for church that evening, though it was many years before he told the story to his parents.

The Reverend Graves must have known about the old Great Northern Railway coach in a place called Tokio, North Dakota, which was retired and serving as a Catholic chapel during the 1930s. For some time, a trumpet was used to call the congregation to mass, though later the GN also contributed a locomotive bell.

Incidentally, if thoughts of the Reverend Graves's rather opulent railroad manor excites you more than owning a simple caboose, such cars *are* still available, for those with enough money. Like old paintings and antiques, some of the most elaborate railway cars ever built are now and again offered for sale, though not exactly in galleries and exhibition places. Often restored to immaculate condition, these cars can cost in the hundreds of thousands of dollars, not counting the moving.

Of course, some can be found much cheaper, if they need a lot of work. Just a couple of years ago I saw a rare classic on the Burlington Northern, in Bonners Ferry, Idaho. Disguised in flat red paint and lost in the midst of a work train, the pedigree of this car was instantly recognizable by two distinct, outside features—an oval, leaded window midway on each side, and fancy brass railings (albeit unpolished) around an open platform observation deck at the rear. This meant that the car had once served as a first-class means of travel, though I don't know what has happened to it since.

A work train on the Chessie system was recently found to include a century old classic originally built for top railway executives. After serving as a shabby crew car, this one has suddenly become a protected celebrity; museum residence is assured upon its retirement, according to present-day officials.

THE MAHARAJAH'S PRIVATE CAR

If the parlor car of the Reverend Graves makes my old caboose sound kind of plain, how do we describe the private coach built for the maharajah of Indore in 1936. Perhaps the "Rolls Royce of Rail Cars" would be appropriate. For $77,500 (Amtrak would consider *that* a bargain price, today, for just a plain coach!), a British firm delivered to his highness what was described as "the world's most elaborately equipped railway car."

This small-scale, mobile palace-on-railroad-wheels measured only ten by sixty-eight feet, but weighed more than fifty tons. There were many places it couldn't even travel, because the tracks could not bear its weight. Its body was of heavy steel, lined with asbestos and papered with fine parchment. Virtually bullet-proof, it was also well insulated and almost unbelievably opulent.

The maharajah's bedroom was equipped with handcarved furniture of white sycamore, including a bed five feet wide. The luxurious bathroom had a hot and-cold shower. A stately drawing room was used for meetings, while a nearby kitchen was equipped with refrigerators, stone sink and stone cupboard. Think of the fresh fruit and vegetable salads that must have been prepared on those swaying counters!

For his smaller children, the maharajah had the car equipped with a nursery that most kids would see only in their fantasies. They had their own bathroom, and there was a sleeping room for their nurse. Imagine being one of those kids, seeing beautiful but squalid India through the lacy curtains of your father's own railway car. . . .

The British had a heck of a time just getting this car out of their country. It was built for India's broad-gauge railways, which made it too wide for Britain's narrower tracks. Railway agents made up a complicated timetable allowing it to be towed to the harbor at Liverpool without having to meet opposing trains, en route. At every tunnel and bridge the car had to be shifted toward one side of its wheels in order to avoid scrapings and collisions. This car is conceivably still rolling in India, a country whose railways operate with a lot of basic technology left from an earlier industrial age, including a heavy reliance on steam power.

TWO GIRLS ALONE IN A CABOOSE

Now hold on; this is *not* the X-rated part of this book! It's a clean story about two young ladies, Margaret Whittemore and Lillian Steinmeyer, who bought their own caboose back around 1943. This was down near Topeka, Kansas, and the car was an old "four-door model" built for the Santa Fe Railroad in 1913.

Both ladies had a bit of railroading in their blood. Lillian, for instance, was a teacher by trade, but she traveled extensively on trains in her free time. One summer she worked as Comptometer operator in the Santa Fe freight auditor's department. It may have been inside those probably stuffy offices that she got the fever to move out into a caboose. And the thing was parked way out in the woods, too, right alongside a river. Many cabooses have ended up as cabins for those who yearn to be in the outdoors; theirs was one of them.

Margaret's railroad work involved drafting for the Santa Fe's mechanical engineering department—making plans showing the engines, cars, nuts and bolts of railroading. I can see how a bachelor lady of that kind would consider a caboose to be a pretty practical place.

Actually, this old caboose that they moved into was already owned by somebody else, a mother and son—an elderly mother, a grown-up son. You have to expect these odd match-ups, since no ordinary family would fit into a caboose. This old lady's son was a railfan named Chester Boggs; it was he who started this caboose on its second life. He'd found it in the Topeka freight yards in 1937, ready to be scrapped. By then, the old four-door style of cabooses had been largely outlawed because of dangers associated with using the two side doors. Boggs bought the car for forty dollars!

The old caboose was moved by truck and crane to a wooded

site along the banks of the Wakarusa River, where Boggs and his mother moved into it. Gradually, they turned the nine- by thirty-foot rectangle into a neat little country home, landscaped on the outside and domesticated within.

In recent years, because of the availability of motels and taxis, railroad crews have not needed to use their cabooses as homes, so they are often furnished to look more like mobile headquarters for work gangs. But the Santa Fe caboose that Boggs bought had four double-deck sleeping bunks, each measuring three feet by six. That's enough to sleep eight men (in the days *before* women's liberation, I hasten to add). That's quite a crew for any train, making me wonder what other service this caboose was meant for. (Our cabooses, incidentally, have three bench beds each, for the conductor and his two brakemen. *Engine* crews didn't use the cabooses, but stayed in rooms at the stations or in nearby hotels.)

Boggs removed some of these bunks to make space for a sitting and living room, though he left two sets of upper and lower berths. Up in the cupola, he also removed some of the seats, creating more space and light for the kitchen which was directly below (ours have cupboards directly below, on both sides, four on one and three on the other. Lots of space, which I have filled with lots of "stuff," even though some part or another is inevitably prone to leaking).

The two young ladies bought this place from the mother of Boggs, after he was drafted into World War II. They repainted the interior in bright colors, added cheery curtains and covered the walls with maps and posters. In cool weather, they cooked over a two-lid, pot-bellied stove. In warm weather, they moved outdoors to a stone oven, which they had built under the trees.

Said Margaret enthusiastically, "Little did I dream a few years back that I'd own something like this. The only other caboose-house in the whole state of Kansas that I know of belongs to the Girl Scouts, over in Moundridge."

So, "girls" of the 1980s, there's your precedent to go out and get yourself a caboose!

CHAPTER FOUR

I've Been Workin' on the Railroad

The wind was high and the steam was low.
The train was heavy and hard to tow.
The coal was dirty and full of slate;
And that's the reason we came in late.

—ANONYMOUS ENGINEER

Wish I could say that opening poem offers a description of my days of working on railroad locomotives! If so, it would mean I'd been aboard coalburners and steamers—engines of romance—instead of just "plain old diesels." I used to travel far and wide in search of steam scenes to photograph, but I hardly ever brought my camera with me during my two and a half years of riding in diesel cabs. The new scenes were too common and ordinary in the early sixties, when antique operations could still be found surviving in isolated pockets of North America.

"You worked in the cab of an E-8?" a young fellow with a fuzzy, blond mustache asked me a few years ago. The E-8 was the Cadillac of 1940s and '50s diesels; it was even built by the Electro Motive Division of General Motors. Most E-8s have now been replaced, scrapped; barely a handful are left in service (running mainly on commuter lines in the eastern United States). To some young railfans, having "fired" one almost puts me in a league with old steam engineers.

With all the great railroad stories that have been committed to paper over 150 years, it's debatable whether much more of interest can be added by a fellow like me, who, fresh out of high school, spent only a few brief seasons on diesels.

But if my time on E-8s qualifies me to entertain a few railfans, then my experience as a locomotive fireman should at least allow me to pay some sort of tribute to that now defunct occupation. In 1962, after almost a century of young fellows trading school desks for the left-hand seats of locomotives, I was among the last of them to do it. Who knows how many tens of thousands there were before me, including one of my own grandfathers.

In spite of my life-long interest in trains, it's odd that for a long time I thought railroad work was only for older men, especially jobs aboard locomotives. The stereotype image of elderly "Engineer Bill," handlebar mustache flying in the wind, must have been learned from movies and folk stories. However, there actually were periods following both world wars during which railroads had so much business and hired so many men that they didn't need new personnel for many years after. It may be that the stereotype was common then, though there have certainly been many young engineers during other periods, some as young as sixteen and eighteen (or, in rare cases, even younger).

At any rate, my enthusiasm for trains never got me to think seriously about "going railroading" until my friend Mike Kessler called and said that's what he'd done. The Southern Pacific had hired him as a fireman on switchers, in their Los Angeles yards. He set my enthusiasm off like a time bomb, even though I hadn't noticed it ticking. Not only did train-riding appeal to my pleasure senses, a good-paying job in the middle of an out-of school, out-of-work summer was just what I'd been looking for.

But when I phoned the SP, they had enough men, as did the competing Santa Fe. That left Union Pacific—the third of Southern California's "big three" railroads—and I happened to have a couple of well-placed friends there. It never hurts to have a guide or two when trying to enter a big building with many doors and hallways.

I came by my inside connections honestly, having provided some Union Pacific officials with valuable information after one of their local trains was derailed and wrecked near my home. One crewman was seriously injured when the locomotive and several cars went down an embankment at a junction switch. I overheard a neighborhood "tough guy" brag about having sawed the lock and set the switch in the middle.

My tip was followed by his confession, which got me two official business cards, along with an offer to visit the company's properties, especially after it was noticed that I carried a camera.

A phone call to one of those officials that summer, about a year after the derailment, got me an invitation to "come up and fill out an application." Union Pacific's offices and yards were located in East L.A., bisected overhead by the Long Beach Freeway and bordered on the sides by a large Mexican community. As soon as I handed back the paperwork, I was accepted as a student switchman, sent to the company doctor for examination, then ordered to spend ten days learning the whys and hows of freight yard switching. The job didn't sound nearly as glamorous as locomotive fireman, but at least it *was* a job, and it was still a railroad, besides.

After I warmed my hands on a little glass vial (if you know what I mean!), a Chinese doctor at the company clinic came into my room and said, very matter-of-factly, "Splead cheeks, please." I figured it was time to see if I had tonsillitis or rotten teeth, so I opened my mouth. Only when he said again, "Splead cheeks, please," and slapped my behind, did I realize what he actually wanted. After that, I was glad he was at the other end, so he wouldn't see my red face. But I did pass the medical.

The first thing a new railroad employee has to learn is "the book," meaning the company rules. He is heavily indoctrinated until he understands that these must be obeyed to the word! On them depends all the safety and success of various train movements. Even a small infraction could lead to dangers and deaths. I, and five other high-school-age newcomers, quickly realized that there was no fooling around to be done here.

The more exciting part of our student education took place out in the yard, where we got hands-on lessons around trains and tracks: Don't step on the tops of rails; you could slip and twist your ankle. Don't climb under or between cars; they might start rolling at any time. When getting off a moving train (all day long, as working switchmen), always put your inside foot on the ground first; if you stumble it will push you away from the tracks.

The big test of these outdoor lessons was whether we could walk along the tops of moving trains. Each of us had to do it, one or two at a time. The trains weren't just moving slowly in one direction, either; they stopped and performed switching while we were underway. We'd go from front to back, then up front again, ten or fifteen cars. I'll be darned if I counted then, though I learned later that it helps if you do. Sometimes a particular car had to be located and checked while the train was underway, making it imperative to know the right one.

"Anybody that don't have the guts for this better speak up now," announced our instructor in a deep, booming voice. He was a heavy-set old switchman, selected for the job by officials (rumor had it he was a company spy, a "brown-noser"). He never climbed up on top of the cars himself, but told us very clearly how to do it. Some years after this, roofwalks were removed from all mainline cars and warnings were stenciled on the cars saying, "Employees must not ride on top."

Old-time brakemen could have filled many books with stories about heat, wind, storms and blizzards as experienced on the tops of rocking and bucking old freight cars. More than a few didn't even survive the challenges long enough to think about writing books.

It turned out all six of us "had the guts," but only four really needed them. I and one other got called to the main office just when our student trips were completed. "You two fellows want to hire out as firemen, instead?" we were asked. Holy cow, I thought, immediately answering "Yes," before the offer could be withdrawn. That same night I was already heading down the main line aboard the locomotive of a freight. No more getting on and off moving cars all day and night for me, nor the constant lining of switches and uncoupling of cars; no, not even a stroll on the roof would I need to take anymore! Instead, I became copilot of the whole darned train. Let me tell you about a couple of my most memorable experiences.

OFF THE END OF THE DOCK

It happened during the night shift, but was never officially recorded. A lot went on, down at the L.A. harbor, many things whose details were never fully known. In fact, some things even went on *way* down *in* the harbor . . .

One of my longest assignments as a fireman for the Union Pacific Railroad was working the graveyard shift at the L.A. harbor, switching cars around warehouses, factories and docks. Big, quiet ships; dark, brooding waters; they helped to make it kind of an eerie job. There was always a lot for us to do, some of it in fairly dangerous places, where tracks made tight curves and ran close to the water. Also, there were numerous unsavory characters who seemed to wander through the dark.

This particular night followed a warm and pleasant Saturday. I had slept all morning, till past noon, then driven down to the beach and lain in the sunshine for a couple of hours, enjoying the coastal "scenery," especially such as had two legs. Mother had supper ready at six, when I got home, after which I dressed up in my "fancy duds" and went back down to the beach, where I liked frequenting a young people's dance place. This was during my last teenage year.

The dance was really swinging; I had a couple of girls smiling and talking; the night was going well. Then I suddenly realized it was time to start my drive to the harbor, several dozen miles away. It was a few minutes past midnight when I pulled up to the dilapidated station that served as the harbor railroad office. Train crews booked in at one end of the pale colored structure. Inside was a crew room full of well-worn chairs, its faded, green-painted walls almost totally covered with bulletins and notices.

"My" crew didn't look too cheerful when I came dashing in

late. One of them muttered, "It's about time." I hurriedly stamped my name in the log book, then followed them outside, where we all climbed up into an elderly engine parked on the tracks. The black, greasy thing chortled and burbled with such peculiar sounds that crews knew immediately it had been built by Baldwin, a famous steam-engine manufacturer. A few years after this, Baldwin became among the first diesel engines to go, replaced mostly by GM products. The regular engineer on this job was a slim, jovial Southerner who spoke with a drawl. I found him easy to get along with. We made many jokes, talked about all manner of subjects and looked the other way whenever one of the switchmen came aboard with booty.

Usually it was food or clothing, taken from one of the warehouses. Sometimes they brought cases of soap from the Boraxo factory, where we switched cars, or stalks of green bananas, whenever a banana boat was in. Samples of this stuff were always being given to us, in return for "seeing nothing." I never felt comfortable about it, but as the "youngster," I was shy to speak up to the crew, so I just accepted the bribery. On this night, the regular engineer had booked off, and I got stuck with an unfriendly relief man. I hadn't time to change into my work clothes, though I brought them up into the engine with my handbag.

When I got to my seat, the new engineer gave me the once-over, *very slowly;* I could tell immediately that he didn't approve. Starting at my pointed, ankle-high "fruit boots," he moved his cold stare up to my green "pegger" pants, then to my collarless "Nehru jacket," until finally they came to rest behind my ears, where my hair reached about halfway to my shoulders. No big deal nowadays, but it was then, in the early sixties.

"She-it!" he declared. "Are *you* my fireman?" It was a question wanting no answer. To my silent stare he added "Hmpfff!" then turned away and got himself settled on the seatbox. My teenage mind no doubt thought up several equally sarcastic replies, but I kept them to myself. The man was about as old as my father; his kind of attitude was common in society at that time, especially at work places. It seldom bothered me.

Since this engineer wasn't regularly assigned to the harbor, he was given extra mileage pay to drive down from L.A. He worked for UP, just like I did, but the rest of our crew didn't. Two came from Southern Pacific (as did our Baldwin engine), while the third was a Santa Fe man. We were all "subcontracted" to the Harbor Belt Line Railroad, which had no crews of its own, but used those of the three big railroads it served. Our paychecks carried an "HBL" imprint.

This relief engineer's disdain for me did not bode well for the coming night's work. Up in Union Pacific's big East L.A. yard, an engineer could get along pretty well without a fireman, even though this was before radios and walkie-talkies had replaced hand signals. But down at the harbor, curves and obstructions often hid all the crew members from an engineer's sight, so that he had to depend on verbal orders passed by his fireman based on signals given over on the fireman's side. But the two enginemen had to get along halfway decently in order for this to be a good working arrangement. It got pretty hard when the two were mad at each other.

There was another drawback to the makeup of our working crew that night. The three ground men were headed by a rowdy Italian named Palumbo (not his real name), who seemed to have little regard for property, or even human life. He traveled to work on a chromed chopper, wearing black leather and heavy boots. He was right out of the movies, although he wore no chains or medals. He was friendly enough, yet he always had this "don't-give-a-damn about-nothing" attitude that made me uncomfortable. He talked quite a bit, mostly about ordinary things, when not outside doing switching work. I couldn't figure out how he got to be a foreman, since that job entailed some bit of responsibility. To me, Palumbo fit the SP stereotype described among rival UP crews, who claimed the other line had lower qualifications.

The main problem in working with Palumbo was that he gave sloppy signals that sometimes caused us to back strings of cars into standing ones at too fast a speed. It made our job in the cab unpleasant, because we were always waiting to be jolted off our seats. That night, this happened to me twice. The second time I went down, it cost me part of a good sandwich, not to mention my pride, there, in front of that smirking engineer. A sore wrist came from trying to block the fall, which was the final straw. Under my breath I swore I'd find a way to get even with that foreman.

My chance came unexpectedly about a half hour later, while we were performing a maneuver called "kicking cars." Although against the rules down on crowded harbor tracks, it saved us from having to run the engine up and down various sidings. On a curve ahead of us, we had about twenty boxcars, which we were separating onto three different tracks. By the glare of industrial lights, I could see clearly down to the ends of *two* of these tracks, which were slowly filling up with cars. The third track went out of sight behind a huge warehouse, next to which was docked a foreign freighter, its massive bow dominating the nearby landscape.

The boss of the locomotive didn't need to see the train in order to picture what was going on. He simply released the brakes, pulled back on the throttle slowly, then got us moving faster and faster.

At this point, the foreman—or one of his men—would "pull the pin" on the lead car, thus allowing the knuckle of its coupler to open. Then the foreman would swing his lantern from side to side, in a low arc, which I would translate to the engineer as "that'll do!" The engineer would then shut off the throttle and apply the brakes. As we slowed to a halt, the uncoupled car would keep rolling down onto the track for which it was intended, usually coupling up to the first car it encountered.

We made several of these "kicks," during which I was amazed at how fast the foreman sometimes let the cars get rolling before he called for us to stop. Even five miles an hour is fast when two loaded boxcars hit, believe me! Several times, I heard hefty banging sounds, audible even with all the noise of our rumbling and rattling diesel engine. All sounds were amplified even more by the wall created by the combination of the warehouse and the ship, directly behind. I thought about damage to the goods or to the cars themselves; but a fireman was not expected to interfere with the switch foreman's work.

Just to be ornery, one time I decided to ignore one of the foreman's stop signals, after he got us to kick a car down the hidden track at a pretty good speed. I looked aside when the stop signal was given, saying nothing to the engineer, who kept open the throttle. By the time the foreman realized his signal had been missed, plus the time it took him to give it again, we were moving along at a speed that might have been approaching fifteen; awfully fast for dead-end tracks! I expected there'd be sparks when that uncoupled car hit whatever was parked down that further track. But boy, was I in for a surprise!

It was later said that the car carried manufactured goods bound for Hawaii, going aboard the ship that was docked. It was the *first* car to go down that track, near the ship; we had pulled all the other cars out of there earlier. As a result, the well-oiled wheels of our kicked boxcar were allowed to roll merrily along, unobstructed, right to the end of the dock! At that point, its momentum was such that the steel buffer just "joined the parade," as if it were a loaf of bread. In other words, the whole works left hardly any sign that it had been there, as it went off the end of the dock and dove down into the murky waters below, just a few yards from the big ship.

None of this was known to us inside the cab until the foreman stormed in, looking "fit to kill." He tried to say several things at once, but nothing coherent came out for a while. Eventually he managed to spit out some of the facts, practically every word tied to the next with a piece of profanity.

Yet, before the night was over, he withdrew all the facts. "You don't know nothin' about any missin' boxcar!" he ordered us in a threatening voice. "Nothin', you understand? You didn't see nothing; you didn't hear nothing! OK?" Yeah, sure boss, I figured; we didn't see nothin'. What's up, anyways?

An official investigation followed, during which we each had to submit signed statements concerning the event. The engineer and I played "hear no evil, see no evil" to its fullest, writing that on the night in question we had been at all times aboard our engine, running it according to signals given from the ground. Nothing more came of the matter after that; not even the foreman got fired!

THE MIDNIGHT SWITCHER

A somewhat similar incident took place in the yards at Las Vegas, Nevada, though it came much closer to costing me my job. That time I was with an old and experienced crew who got pretty worked up about the accident we had.

The "Midnight Switcher" at Las Vegas was a much different sort of train than the "Midnight Special" of song. For instance, it wouldn't have inspired a fellow to write about "Atlanta Women," nor about being "chain-gang bound," though the song line, "you'd better not gamble," could have made a suitable motto. Every night, from about three to four-thirty in the morning, we took off from the "Midnight Switcher" for "beans"—railroad talk for "coffee and grub." One of the crew would drive, while the rest of us rode in his car, always to visit the twenty-four-hour downtown of Las Vegas, where we'd pass the time in one of the casinos.

As I recall, being eighteen was too young to legally gamble, but there were no ID checks, especially on a bunch of railroaders at four in the morning. We took turns between courses to feed loose change to the slot machines. One night, I ended up with a pocketful of quarters, which made me feel giddy about the "sport." The next night, I went back to the casino and spent a couple of hours before going to work, figuring to try my luck at the card tables. Blackjack became my game; in an hour I turned a twenty dollar stake into nearly three hundred dollars. "Lucky Adolf," I fancied myself for a short while, sitting there among all sorts of well-heeled folks, no one yet asking my age. I bet they never guessed that within an hour I'd be the fireman of the local yard switcher. What's more, I bet none of them cared, though they took all my money just the same. Every last dollar of it! The others in our crew laughed when I told them, though I was kind of glum about it for a couple of days.

Las Vegas was the last place on the Union Pacific system that I wanted to be that winter of '62. When work slowed down in the fall, I started going to college. A union agreement with the company allowed us to "book off" fourteen days at a time, provided we then "book on" for at least one.

We got no pay for these days off, but we could do whatever we wanted. When traffic picked up, and we were needed again, only medical excuses were accepted for the fourteen days off.

The railroad ran short of men at Las Vegas; I was next on the assignment list; so that job was settled for me. Except that my college classes were in Long Beach, California, and the job was a couple of hundred miles away. I had arranged the classes to take up only four days a week, giving me three-day weekends. By cutting my attendance even further, here and there, I was able to work four or five days in Las Vegas, then come back for a few days of school. Surely, I was the only student on campus with such a crazy commuting schedule. I made these frequent round-trips by train, using free company passes to ride the eastbound *City of St. Louis* and the westbound *City of Los Angeles*.

The worst part about this being "force assigned" to Las Vegas was that the midnight switch job was absolutely the most boring. We spent all night going up and down long, dark tracks, out on the hot, open desert. A mile or two away, we could see neon lights of air-conditioned nightclubs beckoning to us. One showed the time and temperature, which was sometimes over 100 degrees in the middle of the night. It was often hot and dusty in our cab, and I got terribly sleepy. The noise and constant movement only kept part of me awake, while diesel fumes and creosote from hot ties gave me headaches.

Fortunately, a couple of factors about this desert job kept it from being a total disaster. For one, we had a nice GP-9 road engine, which traveled smoothly and quietly compared to the noisy and wobbly switchers that generally prowled the yard tracks in L.A. For another, the kindly engineer allowed me to spend part of the night running this well-bred machine. My feelings, each time, were like those of a twelve-year-old getting a chance behind the wheel of the family car.

I was at the throttle the night we cost the company a lot of trouble. In fact, the train crew blamed it all on me, though the engineer backed me up and said it was their fault. Not that he actually saw any of it—soundly dozing, as he was, on my usual seat. But from descriptions of the event, he realized just what had taken place; also, I think he felt sorry for me.

Full of eager innocence, I held the shiny throttle firmly in my hand, watching for lantern signals up ahead, as we pushed a couple dozen cars around a long, open curve of track toward some distant warehouses and factories. Unfortunately, I didn't know the layout of the place, having not been to this part of Las Vegas before. My job was somewhat like that of a pilot coming in for a landing only by viewing his control panel and hearing directions from the tower.

There was no problem on our way out to the site, nor with the switching of cars that we did there for the next little while. When a lantern went up and down in the dark, I let off the brakes and pulled back the throttle to move ahead. The size of the up and down movement told me how far we would be moving. A light raised high and held still told me we were approaching the end of a track or else another car. Little flicks to one side said how many car-lengths that obstacle was away. When the lantern light went down and swung from side to side, it meant we should stop. Good engineers made a ballet dance out of this coordination between lamp signals and distant couplings. Beginners like me made a lot of stops too short, else a lot of extra noise!

We ended up taking more cars away from these outlying warehouse tracks than we'd brought in. Slowly, our engine moved further and further out into the bleak, dark desert as we put together our train. At one point, I could no longer see the lamp signals at all, so I had to stop and wait for one of the men to get up on the cars, relaying signals from another man down on the ground.

The tough part for me was the occasional wait of five or ten minutes between movements, having no idea why or what was going on. The constant idling of the diesel's motors quickly made my idling mind grow drowsy, even if I kept my head leaning out from the window as far as I could.

After one particularly long wait I finally saw all three of our switchmen moving their lamps up and down, telling me to "come ahead." I let off the brakes and pulled the throttle back a notch or two. Being a road engine, she did not respond immediately with a move, but first revved her motors a bit. Eventually we got rolling, only to be stopped again, immediately. I shut off the throttle and pulled back the brake valve, though it took some time for the slack to run out of all the couplers and for our momentum to stop the last of the cars.

Soon I got the signal to come ahead again. I could hear the loud banging down the line, as the cars bunched up and took the slack away. Before there was time for our engine to pick up speed, I again got a stop signal, this one much faster than the previous one and coming from all three lanterns. After that, I saw nothing more, as I leaned out the window and waited.

But, my, what a storm of words rose to my ears when those crewmen finally showed up at the head end! Climbing up into the cab, they all three talked, while I tried to make out what they meant. Something about cars out on the desert. . . . The foreman spoke for them when they got inside, all three looking fairly hostile. "How many more blankety-blank cars do you want to throw out there on the desert?" he nearly shouted, while I still couldn't make any sense out of the anger.

Not until they settled down and the engineer got involved did we begin to actually communicate. Apparently, we'd completed our work and had our train all coupled together before this trio took time out to go into the warehouse, to have coffee in its lunchroom. That's when I was trying to stay awake all that time, by myself. When I finally saw their lamps giving the first "come ahead" signal, they had actually just been walking beside the back of the train, heading up toward the engine while talking to each other and carelessly swinging their lit lamps. By the time they got me stopped, the slack running out was enough to make the last car kick the big steel bumper post right off the end of the track.

I never got it clear if part of the car itself went off that first time or not. But it did, the second time! Eventually, the count was *two* cars off, along with the front wheels of a third one. My second start had caught them so much by surprise—they thought the first one was crazy enough—that the train moved some distance before they got it stopped. Apparently, it *then* had dawned on them why I kept moving it, so they put out their lamps and walked up in the dark.

That morning, when I got off work, it appeared likely to be my last stint on the railroad, at least by the way the crew talked, *including* the friendly engineer. He *still* said he'd take my side. The problem was, a recent company bulletin had forbidden engineers to let firemen run the locomotives. This was part of the company's effort to show the public that firemen had no work to perform on diesel engines and could thus be eliminated (as they soon were).

There was a happy tour group at the Las Vegas depot as I walked by, on my way to the bunkhouse for some hours of rest. Their laughter was like salt in a wound; I wasn't feeling very funny. Then, suddenly, my name was called, and I looked to see one of the officials who had helped me get the job in the first place. He was up from L.A., on company business, shaking my hand firmly and asking in a cheerful voice how things were going. I briefly explained why they weren't going too well just then, telling him the true story of my night's mishap. Things must have been going *very* well for him; he told me to go get some sleep and to say no more about the incident. I did as he advised, and that was the end of it; he must have had a talk with someone, though no one ever mentioned it to me.

There was one other benefit to those frequent train trips back and forth to Las Vegas, being a footloose bachelor. Among the passengers were always a few young ladies; on nearly every trip I managed to strike up friendships with one or two of them. Sometimes the visits would develop beyond conversations about parents, schools, or working on the railroad—especially if we were sitting in one of the upstairs domes, after dark, when there weren't many others around.

A couple of these meetings even led to later dates, in Las Vegas, when I was lucky enough to encounter young ladies from there. I had a pretty good thing going with one of them until her dad found out I worked for the railroad. He forbade her to see me after that, saying he knew just how our kind fooled around with women. He had retired the previous year as a conductor from the same railroad!

Bribery was how I finally got out of Las Vegas and back to work in L.A. There was such a crew shortage in the desert that crew dispatchers no longer wanted to let me off to attend my classes. The first time this happened, I persuaded the local company doctor that my throat was sore enough for me to need a few days' rest, but I realized that the next time around such an excuse would be further looked into.

Then I learned that a fireman with more seniority than I had just come back from vacation, with the right to "bump" anyone younger than he for his job. It cost me the previous two weeks' check to bribe that fireman into "bumping" my job. That gave me the same privilege back in L.A., where a younger fireman was working the evening switcher at the city's Union Station passenger terminal. By bumping him, I was able to attend classes all day, yet still be at work by 4 P.M. Besides that, I got to ride an engine all evening around tracks filled with the colorful passenger trains belonging to three different railroads: UP, SP and Santa Fe.

Eventually *I* got bumped off that ideal job, too, so I moved to another, and that was the way it went for several more seasons. Union Pacific had over fifty different around-the-clock switching jobs going in L.A., each with a crew of five. Bumping changed the names of these five regularly, except for those of the more senior members, who usually picked the best jobs and settled themselves in.

Young guys like me sort of worked along the edges, now and then getting lucky and catching a local or mainline freight when an older man suddenly booked off. Once, my name even got put up for the *City of St. Louis*, the line's flagship passenger train. A single round-trip would have paid many times the amount I made per day in the yard, but an older fellow bumped me about a half hour before I was to get the official call. Darn; I've always been sorry that I missed that trip.

The nation signed a collective death warrant for locomotive firemen in the fall of 1964, voting on the so-called "featherbedding" proposition. Like cabooses, the job of fireman had a lot of romance and tradition in the public's eye. Besides, none of us wanted to lose our jobs. Yet, I had to admit that, for the majority of my paid time, I did little more than occupy space on some locomotive's second seat. When friends asked me how they should vote on the issue, I told them honestly, "I'd rather not say, since I'm divided about it myself."

A check for $2,100 was my severance pay from UP, and it went a long way to support me through college, since I still lived rent free at home. About the time I started graduate work, the railroad even asked me to come back. Retirements had left them short of engineers, so they figured their former firemen would make better trainees than new fellows, off the streets. But by then I knew my inner self would never be happy working with machines, nor with living around cities. Later, when I moved to the Canadian Rockies, I thought I was leaving behind my railroad involvements for good! Caboose homes were not at all in my plans!

THE MIDNIGHT MAIL

A headlight flashes through the night,
   A shower of sparks shoots high;
A swish, a roar, a streak of light,
   And then the train is by,
While faint and fainter comes the wail
   Of whistle from the Midnight Mail.

Night after night, year after year,
   In starlight, snow or rain,
I lay awake until I hear
   The passing of this train.
And never have I known to fail
   The whistle of the Midnight Mail.

I've journeyed far through foreign land;
   On trains renowned for charm,
But none to me seemed quite so grand
   As this one through our farm;
For every night I missed the tale
   Of whistle from our Midnight Mail.

And so, content to live am I
   Beside the right-of-way,
With one fond wish—that when I die
   I want my bones to lay
Right here beneath the friendly hail
   Of whistle from the Midnight Mail.

—ANONYMOUS, c. 1920.

CHAPTER FIVE

Notes from a
Family Freight Yard

One evening as the sun went down
  And the jungle fire was burning,
Down the track came a hobo hiking
  And he said, "Boys, I'm not turning,
I'm headed for a land that's far away,
  Beside the crystal fountain.
So come with me: we'll go and see
  The Big Rock Candy Mountain.

In the Big Rock Candy Mountain
  There's a land that's fair and bright,
And the handouts grow on bushes,
And you sleep out every night;
Where the boxcars all are empty,
  And the sun shines every day;
Where there's birds and bees
  And the cigarette trees,
Where the lemonade springs
  And the bluebird sings—
In the Big Rock Candy Mountain.

In the Big Rock Candy Mountain
  All the cops have wooden legs;
The bulldogs have rubber teeth,
  And the hens lay soft-boiled eggs;
Where the farmers' trees are full of fruit,
  And the barns are full of hay,
Oh, I'm bound to go
  Where there ain't no snow,
Where the rain don't fall,
  And the wind don't blow—
In the Big Rock Candy Mountain.

In the Big Rock Candy Mountain
  You never change your socks,
And the little streams of alcohol
  Come trickling down the rocks;
Where the brakemen have to tip their hat,

And the railroads pull their blinds.
Oh, a lake of stew, and whiskey, too;
    You can paddle around in a big canoe—
In the Big Rock Candy Mountain.

In the Big Rock Candy Mountain
    All the jails are made of tin,
And you can walk right out again
    Just as soon as you are in;
Where there ain't no short-handled shovels,
    No axes, saws or picks;
Where they hang the Turk
That invented work—
In the Big Rock Candy Mountain.''

—"HAYWIRE MAC"*

A few winters ago, our family was host to what must surely
have been the first traditional native ceremony ever held inside
a railroad caboose. In fact, I haven't come across stories involving
cabooses with any kind of religious practices, so our gathering
may have been a first in a much broader context (though the ghost
of some old Bible-pounding conductor must have shuddered once
or twice in the closets when our ancient ritual began).

In tribal circles, even today, some families periodically sponsor certain traditional prayer meetings and ceremonies that last
all night. A leader, wise in these ways, is hired to sing the many
ancient songs and to perform other rituals that are symbolic of a
faith in the powers of nature and the universe. A number of
invited participants join in the prayer and singing, as well as the
smoking of pipes. Many of the songs represent various initiations
that the singers have gone through, according to the tribal cus-
toms. Among the 25,000-member Blackfoot Confederacy, some
of these handed-down ways are still being faithfully practiced.
The ceremony we held is like an important recital of the Blackfoot
tribal legacy.

On this particular occasion, we expected a dozen or more
friends and relatives from their reserve homes in Alberta. Know-

*Harry McClintock, the singing brakeman, a popular author of rail fiction.

ing that our small family home would make the event rather crowded and awkward, we decided to host it inside what we call "the kids' caboose," CP Rail's No. 436663, a 1918 model. This car had as its previous owners a local civic group, which had planned to use it for tourist functions, before it went broke. They had already stripped out some of the interior, leaving the main room of the caboose almost bare. This was perfect for the type of seating customarily used on these ceremonial occasions— sitting cross-legged, on cushions, backs against the walls, forming a circle (or in this case a U) around a fire (our woodburning stove).

The crackling stove not only warmed us and a big pot of tea, but its fire also provided glowing coals with which our ceremonial leader frequently lit incense made with bits of sweetgrass (which grows nearby in the summertime). Sponsor of the very sacred Sun Dance ceremonies, and a noted elder among the Blackfoot people, Joe Crowshoe was glad for the opportunity to take part in our unusual "first." He mentioned the old railroad car several times in his fervent prayers, asking that it be filled with good spirits.

The first Blackfeet who rode on trains were brave warriors and chiefs, sometimes with wives and children, who left their wild buffalo plains in the latter part of the nineteenth century to travel east, mostly on government business, to Washington, D.C., or to Ottawa. The earliest of these had to travel good distances by steamboat before they even reached railroad tracks. *"Ishtsi-aenna-kah-siew,"* they said, meaning "steam wagon." They were impressed, but far too proud to become terror stricken, as some silly cartoons in those times suggested.

Ironically, one of the larger Blackfoot family groups that traveled across America by train, back in those earlier years, brought with them a tribal medicine bundle that is now in the keeping of Joe Crowshoe and his family. The keeper that time had a prophetic vision one night, while sleeping beside it in his berth; he saw the train running off from the tracks.

The next morning, the old man was much concerned for the

group's safety, for, in accordance with native beliefs, such dreams are not to be taken lightly. The interpreter was sent to tell the conductor about the dream, though we don't know just how that man reacted. He apparently said that the train had to keep to its schedule. The Indians shook their heads in dismay, saying they would stop it at once, if they were in charge. Having a car to themselves on the train, the devout group decided to perform a ceremony right there, with the same bundle that had inspired the dream.

Imagine the surprise among everyone aboard, first, when they learned about the ceremony and, later, when the train actually did derail! The engine and a number of cars turned over, but the rear of the train, including the special car of tribal people, remained on the tracks.

DERAILMENT AT HOME

We've only had one derailment ourselves, here in the family "freight yard," but it had nothing to do with the ceremony, and it came without warning or helpful dream. Still, for a collection of permanently parked old cars, it was a rather unusual occurrence. Here's what happened that time.

For several seasons, I watched with dismay as one end of my caboose sank slowly lower and lower. In building our short piece of track, with a limited number of salvaged old ties, I had inadvertently left a big space right under one of the five-ton sets of wheels. This was causing the old branchline rails to bow, thus putting great stress on that particular spot. It got so bad that the kids started coming to visit so they could let their toy cars roll, by themselves, *down* my floor!

Because of our remote location, we have a four-wheel drive truck, which I figured was strong enough to nudge my caboose ahead just a few inches, where all the wheels would find better support. Accordingly, I went to the caboose's emergency kit (under one of the bunks) and got out a tow chain (railroad size, with links about the size of my hand!). I hooked this from the caboose coupler to the bumper of my truck, then put the truck in low gear and slowly crept forward until the chain stretched tight.

I had handed a crowbar to an artist friend who happened to be visiting with us. He was supposed to put it under a wheel, to stop the car at just the right spot, *should* it cooperate and move forward at all. Keep in mind, I was trying to tow a total of twenty-five tons, using only our family truck.

The journal boxes must have been greased up really well from our final journey; I hardly even noticed when the caboose's heavy wheels started turning. From the changing sound of the truck's motor, I sensed that we had a load, but nevertheless we just kept going at about the same rate. I expected a signal; when none came, after a few feet, I stopped. To my horror, I saw in the rearview mirror that the car was still rolling. "Use the crow bar," I yelled, quickly putting the truck back into gear to get out of the way.

Then I noticed that the fool had thrown the bar down and was running away! He later said that, when he tried stopping the car, it had just pushed the crow bar ahead on the shiny steel track. At any rate, for a few moments there was nothing any of us could do except stare helplessly, as the caboose rolled to the end of the track. I recall hoping the darned thing wouldn't turn over on its side.

Luckily, it came to a shuddering halt as soon as the first pair of heavy, flanged wheels dove into soft ground. I immediately hooked the chain to the other end of the caboose and tried dragging that twenty-five-ton hulk back up those few inches of dead-end rail. But this time the family truck refused to accept its role as honorary locomotive. Heavy-duty caboose jacks were not among the stock items in my closets when I got this car. Also, I couldn't afford to hire a crane for such a minor job. Just to bring one out here would have cost $100 each way. Instead, for the next few months, those derailed wheels sat as sort of a symbol of defiance from bygone days, an embarrassment to me whenever we had company. The usual question was, "Hey, how'd you accomplish that?''

ENGINEER "SPIKE" CARSON

Rescue from this caboose predicament came from a true hero, an old-time steam engineer who'd done his share of putting railroad wheels on and off tracks. B. A. Carson was known to everyone as "Spike," a suitable nickname he'd carried since his train-loving boyhood in the forests of Vancouver Island. Fascinated by its trains and locomotives, he hung around a local logging operation until one of the old engineers finally invited him for a ride. After that, he went there regularly, gladly relieving the fireman of his work just for the opportunity to feed big chunks of wood through the engine's firebox door.

Engine cabs can be addicting, the boy Spike soon found out. Within a few years, he began his career with steam engines in earnest, working as fireman on trains for the Alberni Pacific Lumber Company. He stayed with the outfit until 1952, when it was shut down in favor of trucks. By that time he had become a locomotive engineer and an inside mechanic. This was on a railroad outfit whose crews did a lot of the maintenance on their own engines.

Spike became a real nuts-and-bolts kind of railroader. You could have locked him in a big shed for a year, supplied him with all the tools and parts, and he would have had an engine built by the end. Not only that, he would have probably fired it up and run it pretty much by himself, too. Getting my pair of caboose wheels back on the track was no more than a couple of friendly chuckles for him. Sometimes when he was here I wished I had a pile of steam-engine parts, even to build just a small one . . .

Good steam engineers were a dime a dozen on Vancouver

Island back in the 1950s, when several big logging railroads were shut down in favor of trucks. Spike recognized reality and became a log truck driver, himself. The only reminder of his locomotive days that he kept in his truck was a cord hanging from the cab roof with which to blow the signals, but now they came from his truck's airhorns instead of from chiming steam whistles.

But some people remembered Spike's skill around steam engines, even after they were all gone out of regular service. In 1977, he was called out of retirement by the Province of British Columbia, which undertook a steam revival program. For the next several years, he helped to overhaul, rebuild and run several vintage steam locomotives, some big and some small, and this became the high point of his life.

Easy-going, sprightly for his age, dressed in striped overalls and cap, Spike became the engineer-hero for all my kids as soon as they met him (when they were still small), just as he did for countless kids—and grown-ups—clear across Canada and even down into the United States. He was sent by the British Columbia provincial government on several long-distance promotion tours, as engineer aboard the province's most famous locomotive, ex-CP engine No. 2860, the "Royal Hudson," which provides the power for trains carrying thousands of passengers every week during the summer along British Columbia's spectacular coast. Spike was in charge of one of railroading's ultimate steam machines, and he loved it.

One of my own greatest thrills on the railroads took place when I rode in the cab of another steam engine with Spike, while we thundered at dusk up the well-laid tracks of CP Rail's line in our Kootenay Valley. After years of wondering what it was like, in years past, to roar by here with steam, Spike made sure that I wasn't disappointed! With throttle well open, the smokestack loudly barking, his right arm resting on the window sill, he called me to his seat and had me stand beside him; then, when we passed directly across the river from our home, he let me pull long and hard on the whistle cord.

For his last few summers, Spike and his wife Joyce came out to our part of the Rockies from their Vancouver Island home, so that the "old fellow" could be in charge of the two steam locomotives that operate at the provincially owned Fort Steele Historic Park. This gave us all a chance to visit, either with Spike on his steam engines or here on my caboose. Also, he was able to give Okan occasional lessons at being a fireman.

The last time we saw Spike, he was running the Fort Steele Shay—a big, husky, geared locomotive of the kind he used to operate on logging railroads. In fact, this one had worked on Vancouver Island not far away from him, at one time. Of all the engines in British Columbia, it was the most fitting one for his farewell run. The summer season ended the day after we saw him, then he and Joyce drove back home. There, his heart gave out in the shower, bringing a peaceful end to a wonderful man.

RAILWAY DAYS OF WORLD WAR II

There was much surprise during the oil crisis of a few years ago, when passenger traffic increased tremendously on North American trains. Many railroads were unable to handle the hordes of people who tried to buy tickets for them. Yet, since that time, North American passenger train services have shrunk much further. There are equipment shortages even in these "better times." Those of you who have been through war times—and know about gas rationing, shortages of parts, and crowded trains—must be wondering what this continent would do in the event of another major war. How would the masses get around?

To give you some idea of how valuable train services *could* again become, here are a few relevant figures: Union Station in Washington, D.C., had 15 ticket windows in regular use *before* the attack on Pearl Harbor in 1941; soon afterward it had 59! There had been 31 ticket sellers, but they became 133. The war also increased the 17 clerks who had handled Pullman and other train reservations to 161. The number of trains in and out of the Washington terminal increased from 246 to 325 a day, and these all became full! Passenger figures went from about 50,000 daily to over 130,000. Similar changes occurred at railroad terminals throughout North America.

During that same war, railfan M. B. Cooke of Jersey City had a heck of a time trying to carry on with his hobby. Wartime traffic brought a lot of old steamers out of semiretirement; it extended the life of many others. Cooke wanted pictures of them all, especially the oldest, knowing they'd be the first to get scrapped right after the war was over. But he was also aware of strict laws about trespassing on railroad property—even stricter ones about photographing military-related places—so he did neither of them; yet he still got into trouble.

It was a photo he took of St. Louis & San Francisco locomotive No. 728, parked nicely in the sun at the Frisco station in Carthage, Illinois, that led him to jail. Who would have imagined trouble coming from snapshots of a simple, old 4-6-0, a turn-of-the-century, everyday-type of locomotive?

After taking his pictures, Cooke drove only two blocks from the station before he was stopped by a city policeman who had been called by a railway agent. He was arrested on suspicion of being a spy, although his developed film showed only the old engine and an equally aged grain elevator. Maybe the elevator was a bomb factory in disguise? They sure treated poor Cooke that way.

City police sent to another town for a Frisco special agent, who got in touch with the FBI and also asked superiors from the railroad forces to come from Kansas City. Cooke was interrogated several times and spent four days in jail, while old steam engines clunked loudly on nearby tracks. It was as if they were making fun of their fan's predicament. In the end, he was sent home with the warning that, if caught photographing Frisco trains again, he would have his camera smashed.

THE RISKS OF RAILROAD PHOTOGRAPHY

You may think we've come a long way in forty years, regarding such situations, but a somewhat similar thing happened to me just a few years ago, not far from famous Banff National Park.

The kids and I had driven to the town of Canmore, Alberta, wanting to photograph the old Canmore Collieries, nestled right under a famous trio of Rocky Mountain peaks called the Three Sisters. It was an incongruous sight; those fantastic, ice-covered crags, hovering over that black, ugly mining hulk, the very symbol of the exploitation of nature. But, *honestly,* we didn't look at it that way, figuring the mine was put there long before modern events wised up society to the threats of destroying our own ecology. I had heard the mine was closing up soon; it had a little locomotive that I wanted to photograph while it was still in operation.

A dirt road led to a gate that had signs giving the name of the company and a warning against trespassing. We figured there would be no harm in driving down the last few hundred yards and asking if we could watch the train. Even if we couldn't stay and watch, we could at least get a couple of pictures on the way. We did that, and no one paid attention to us. At the big mine, I was shy to get out of the truck and ask for permission to stay, so we just turned around and drove away again. A few minutes later, we stopped briefly on the road to visit with friends that we encountered. When they left, a red pickup pulled in behind us and a tall man, who was some kind of guard from the coalmine, walked quickly up to my window and demanded the film from my camera, threatening to have me arrested for trespassing. I gave him some film, though I didn't mention my second camera with most of the pictures. He accused us of being spies for an ecological group and said the mine was being forced to close under just such pressure. Nature groups (rightly) claimed it was polluting a world-famous setting. This guard must have been mad about losing his employment and decided to take it out on us. In doing so, he helped us to recognize the ugliness of the place.

RAILFANNING

The subject of railroad photography brings to mind the category of people known as "railfans." Since, by nature of definition, all present and potential caboose owners *must* be railfans to some extent (unless you don't like your caboose!), it might be well for us to investigate this term just a bit further.

Ordinary folks often have an image of "a bunch of oddballs" they call "rail nuts," who go into ecstasy at the sight of anything to do with trains.

Baseball has its odd characters who go around with sacks of autographed balls. Car collectors sometimes take their favorite vehicles into graves with them. Every hobby has a few participants who are more conspicuous than the rest; train watching is certainly among them.

When asked in high school, I sometimes said my hobby was "ferroequinology," which diffused the chuckles I would have gotten for admitting that I enjoyed riding and photographing trains. My girlfriends usually shrugged, when they found out; my father always said, "Why don't you get interested in something you can make a career out of, like electronics or planes." Too bad he's not around now to see my rail-photo books, or to sway with me for a while in this caboose. I know he would have liked that.

Train riding and train watching has become much more of a family hobby in recent times, along with model railroading. These *used* to be almost exclusively "men's hobbies," back when railroading itself was considered "men's work." Now that we have women engineers and women as roundhouse mechanics, it's no surprise that there are many women railfans, as well. Of course, younger members of a family are easy to convert. Kids have always liked trains; they'll gladly go for rides on them— especially when the "old folks" pay the way! "Railfanning" is fun for all ages and sexes, even though some friends may scoff at it.

The July 1937 issue of *Railroad Stories* (briefly another name for *Railroad Magazine*) presented a history of the so-called "railfan movement." At that time, nearly half its members worked for the railroads themselves. Most railroad companies encouraged this, offering special excursions with interesting trains; some even provided unused stations and railroad cars for club rooms and meeting places.

According to the article, the first railroad line was built and operated in North America by Colonel John Stevens in 1820, on his estate at Hoboken, New Jersey. The first *official* railfan group was organized exactly 100 years later, as the Railway and Locomotive Historical Society, a small group of men who had been documenting railroad history on their own for many years. All three founding members had worked for railroads or railroad equipment manufacturers.

Eleven years later, Freeman Hubbard, in *Railroad Magazine*, started the International Engine Picture Club, which became sort of a hotline for train photographers around the world, claiming a membership of over 10,000 back in the late 1930s.

The best known railfan of this era was the dapper Lucius Beebe, a widely read social columnist who hobnobbed with the rich and famous, inviting them for parties and rides aboard his luxurious private car, the "Gold Coast." For a time, this luxurious conveyance was said to be the last "personally-owned railroad car" running in America. Elaborately furnished in 1890s decor, including a large stone fireplace, this classic rail coach is now part of a popular display at the California State Railroad Museum in Sacramento.

Mr. Beebe wrote numerous books about railroads and about the American West, never missing a chance to voice his disdain for the "modern era" of the forties and fifties. Instead of sneaking around in yards to photograph engines, he always traveled in style, either aboard his own luxurious car or on one belonging to the hosting railroad. Some companies even provided him with special engines, and their crews were ordered to stop wherever this photographer wanted to. Aboard his own car, he was accompanied by a black cook and servant; also, a huge St. Bernard dog with the "cute" name of T-Bone Towser. Always at Lucius Beebe's side was his lifelong valet and fellow train photographer, Charles Clegg, who shot himself not long after Beebe died.

May 16, 1937, was a big day for a lot of American railfans. The International Engine Picture Club sponsored the first major railfan excursion, a steam-filled day in which more than 1,700 railroad enthusiasts took part. Freeman Hubbard and others had gotten the big Pennsylvania Railroad to play host, bringing the whole gang to its gigantic Altoona shops, which had long stood as a mecca of steam locomotives.

The day started out in appropriate style with four long, heavy-weight special trains bringing the enthusiasts to the site. Two of these trains came from New York City with 800 fans aboard; another came from Philadelphia; while a fourth traveled all night from Chicago and Milwaukee. For the rear car of the first train out of New York, the railroad provided its unique track inspection car, whose entire rear wall was glass, providing those who were brave enough to sit close, with a fabulous wide angle view of the Pennsy's multiple-track mainline railroad, going backward and passing by at high speed. On one stretch of line the two special New York trains caught up to each other, with the second one ordered to pass the first. On *its* front was the railroad's latest streamliner—a K-4 class steam engine that really put on a show, with both trains doing over seventy-five miles per hour.

There could be no upstaging of a high-speed railroad adventure like that! One could go back home and relive the thrill of *it,* alone, for a long time. But *this* big crowd spent the rest of that day wandering through sprawling shops overflowing with steam engines of all kinds and sizes. From modern K-4s the list went clear back to Pennsylvania No. 1, a relic from the 1800s that was set out for display. One mainline engine was set up on special rollers that let it be "run" at forty miles per hour while it stayed in one place. Freeman Hubbard later described the event modestly as having been just "a couple of degrees above colossal!"

On that same day, a much smaller group of 162 Pacific Coast railfans met to visit the famous Nevada County Narrow Gauge Railroad, an antique gold-rush short line running on its final bursts of steam. Knowing the end of it was near, officials let the fans have the run of the place, parking all the old engines and cars so they could be best photographed.

During that afternoon, a leisurely excursion was made with a mixed train (a combined passenger and freight train) running twenty-one miles to Grass Valley. Surviving photos of the train show camera-toting railfans hanging *all* over, from the cab to the tender, and tightly packed along three boxcar roofs, in addition to those inside a couple of small wooden coaches. The whole thing looks like a high school graduation party, except that some scenes show the little train crossing a big canyon, high up on a thin, steel bridge.

The word "railfanette" also made news in 1937, when a young lady named Henrietta Carter joined the pioneer, conservative, all-male Railway and Locomotive Historical Society. Within a short time, her example encouraged five more women to join as well. Although in the minority, women have since that time been a growing factor within the railfan movement.

That movement is itself nowadays so full of factions and individual groups that a separate one for women would almost be taken for granted. Gay railfans have their own official group; on a recent streetcar excursion, which they chartered in Toronto, a special request was made for a gay driver, and this was fulfilled.

Henrietta Carter must have been quite a gal. She liked steam engines so much that for both years of the New York World's Fair (1939 and 1940) she played a milkmaid in a daily pageant called "Railroads on Parade," just so she could be around all the trains. She told Freeman Hubbard, afterward, that her biggest regret in life was "not having been born on a caboose." He nominated her as "America's Number One Railfanette." Said he: ". . . You're likely to run into her on almost any railfan excursion out of New York City. Ten to one she'll give you a friendly smile. Sometimes she's clutching a camera, sometimes one of her railroad scrapbacks. On choice occasions, Gypsy-like, she is flaunting a railfan bracelet made from trainmen's uniform buttons, streetcar tokens, a switch key and heaven knows what else—a fetching little novelty, unique and barbaric as Henrietta herself.'' (I can just imagine Freeman, that old smoothy, winking an eye, while some of his puritan readers howled with disgust!)

"Putting up the marker lamps," the conductor of this Norfolk & Western wooden caboose lets the 1940s railroad world around him know that he's on board, his paper work is out and his crew is ready for another train adventure.

Here is the wooden interior of the first steel caboose used on the Lehigh Valley RR in the late 1930s. The crew has just come inside for a break during their night freight run. One brakeman washes his hands, then reads the previous day's paper, while another looks at the darkness outside. The conductor is tending to his paper work at the desk, as usual.

S. K. FARRINGTON PHOTOS

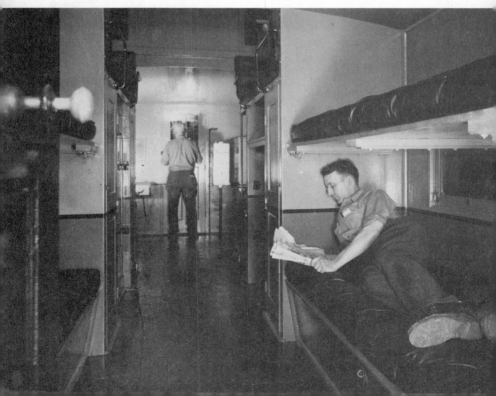

A time-honored tradition, the exchange of "Highball" greetings between engineer and conductor, meaning "all's well" for each other's trains. The steel caboose on this coal train is passing one of the Norfolk & Western's modern and high-powered articulated locomotives, the last to dominate a mainline railroad in the United States (until 1959).

Here's some of that "conductor's paper work." This is what kept the train crew "boss" inside his caboose "office" way more than the rest of the crew. Waybills, time reports, train orders, bad order slips, rule books—the conductor kept them all close at hand, using clipboards, large manila envelopes and a sturdy desk, plus a couple of good pens or pencils. This man has a pretty-well-cushioned seat aboard his wooden caboose on the Norfolk & Western, somewhere down south, in the 1940s. *Below,* The 1910 interior of a brand-new wooden caboose built for some unnamed Western short line. Many railroads built their own cabooses, arranging their design to best suit the intended operation. Some had extra room for freight and passengers, while others were so small that two crewmen felt cramped. This one has room to sleep a crew of four, or else to carry several short-distance passengers.

ROCKY MOUNTAIN FREIGHT TRAIN MUSEUM COLLECTION

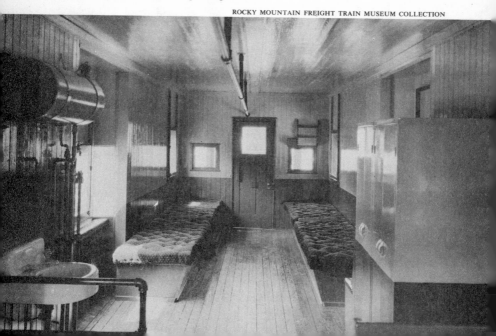

Above, crossing Hadashville trestle on the GWWD, Canada's unique short line, owned by the City of Winnipeg. Trainman Jimmy Landry has his arm out, ready to signal the engineer as soon as caboose 363 reaches the other side. This wooden car is a veteran of CPR mainline service. Ahead of the caboose is the insulated "honey car" for transporting raw sewage. *Below,* veteran of more than forty years on the same railroad, GWWD 44-tonner No. 100 is seen at Manitoba's isolated Indian Bay with its classic shortline freight train, including wooden cars with truss rods and arch-bar trucks. Although the major site of Winnipeg's water operations, Indian Bay has only railroad connections to the "outside world," still served in the late 1980s by vintage trains like this.

Above, any proud town or city with railroad history should have one of these, preferably on wheels and standing on a piece of track. What a nice way to keep alive the mystical lure that cabooses have always had. *Below,* inside this particular tourist information caboose, at an important highway intersection in southern Ontario. A small town can make the space available for clubs and meetings as well.

Above, two fellow caboose owners, Okan and our friend James A. Brown. His former CPR 437187 used to follow freights through the southern Ontario countryside, often on the busy line just a few yards from where it now sits. Jim is a noted Canadian rail photographer, partner in a prestigious rail book publishing firm, owner of the live-steam scale model sitting on tracks next to him, its prototype having often rubbed shoulders with his caboose. And what does this man with so much rail enthusiasm do for a living? He is executive director of railway operations for Ontario's GO Transit, with its very busy trains. *Below,* the KOA of caboose owners seems to be on the Conway Scenic Railroad in New Hampshire, where this lineup of privately owned waycars occupies a scenic back track in the railroad's historic freight yard. Picnic tables, tents and barbecue ovens line the green lawn on the other side of this scene. Maine Central steam engine No. 501 is also a guest, owned and under restoration by a local railfan group.

The year 1910 seems far away from Central Vermont caboose 4011, now that Blanche and Howard Audibert have moved in and done a good deal of redecorating. "I love it," says the lady of the house about her husband's longtime dream come true. Contemporary refinements include sewer and water pipes, electric heat and stove, upstairs and downstairs beds, even a hot and cold shower! ADOLF AND OKAN HUNGRY WOLF PHOTO

CHAPTER SIX

Rail Laws and Handcars

If you're planning to ride a train, maybe you'd better check with your lawyer before you go, to see which of the following unique rail laws are still in effect. For instance:

In Missouri it's against the law to soap a railroad track! Tell your mother that one, especially if she's a fanatic for cleanliness, like some I know. Do you suppose this law was passed to prevent hoboes from bathing on the tracks? If so, you weren't a kid back in the steam days. Near the edge of a typical town, where trains left the railroad yard and headed out on the main line, a good layer of soap on both rails sure did play havoc with those big shiny wheels that struggled to get hold, dragging heavy loads of cars along behind them. Slip, spin; slip, spin. . . . Now do you see why they made a prank like that against the law?

There's probably a similar law enforced against those few railfans who, in order to make the engines spin their wheels, like to pour oil on the rails ahead of excursion steam trains, as they make occasional runs in parts of the country. I've never seen nor done this, preferring to *ask* engineers for a bit of smoke when I want to enliven my pictures. But I hear it makes one heck of a show.

After the mayor has spoken, the band has played and the citizens have taken their snapshots, these railfans wait eagerly for the train to start its triumphant departure from town. A typical one of these steam trains is heavy; once those big steel drivers hit that oil, they have to do a *lot* of cooking before they can get back to real pulling work. The oil has to be in the right place, allowing a bit of room for the train to start up, first. The engine's stack changes from loud, steady shotgun barks to a rapid, machine-gun-like staccato, that can be heard halfway across town (depending on how big the town is). While the driving wheels spin like crazy, the valve gear, rods and other parts look like they will fly right off.

Guys who spread oil on tracks are few, but they do sometimes give the railfan fraternity a bad name. But those who take locomotives for joy rides are much worse, and more dangerous. Iowa will put you in jail just for conspiring to steal a locomotive, so don't even joke around while you're in that state. For the lesser crime of uncoupling a locomotive, Iowa will fine you $1,000.

You generally expect to find the engine of a train coupled on at the front, but just in case, Connecticut has a law making it illegal *not* to have one there. They also want to see a stretcher in every station, which meant quite a few stretchers, at one time, though a stretcher salesman would go broke in that state nowadays, just looking for a station. In the same state, incidentally, streetcar companies had to share the costs of sprinkling water on the streets, although this did their tracks absolutely no good. The same state also ordered fines of $500 for transporting eggs of the browntail moth, so check your coat linings and pockets before you cross its borders.

Arkansas doesn't check you for moth eggs, but they'll fine railroads that let Russian thistles or Johnson grass go to seed along the tracks. I guess train crews in that state are required to study botany; the purpose of this law was mainly to keep livestock from being tempted to graze along the tracks. The more livestock-oriented state of Montana forced its railroads to build sidewalks for cattle to cross trestles. (Careful there, bossy! Don't get spooky while the train rolls by next to you, *way* up here on this narrow trestle!)

For rules on handcars there is Iowa's ordinance making it illegal to *lend* a handcar to a friend! You know a handcar—the kind of thing you go down the tracks on? Probably not a very big problem anymore, since highways are everywhere, along with cars. Back in earlier days, handcars were often the quickest—or only logical—way into town for a railroad man in his time off, which is probably why the law about lending the things came into existence.

But then, they don't even have handcars anymore—at least, not the kind that you pump up and down, or back and forth. Nowadays, they have motorized ones, with heated cabs and soft seats, on which crews whiz along the tracks in style.

While I haven't heard of a handcar being loaned out lately, *we* have one here that was *given* to us by a friend. It is a three wheeler, known as a velocipede, probably built some time in the early 1900s. Since our friend is now a rather high official, with an important Canadian railway company, we won't get too specific about certain details, but . . .

Somewhere on the CP Rail main line through the Canadian Rockies there was an old depot with a small passenger waiting room containing a wooden bench and a cast-iron stove. This was within recent years, when such sights have become rather uncommon. In one corner of this waiting room sat, for the longest time, the disassembled pieces of a freshly-painted velocipede, its yellow wooden seat and black spoke wheels making it a popular destination of small fry accompanying waiting travelers.

One day, I happened to be in that station, waiting for the passenger train, when a nasty little fellow ignored his mother's warning ("Charles, *get* down!) and tumbled off, headfirst, instead. As a result of his lusty hollers, everyone in the station rushed to aid in the emergency, which amounted to no more than soothing the ruffled ego of a nasty boy in the arms of his I-told-you-so mother. As the stationmaster walked away I heard him mutter to another employee, "If the superintendent don't get rid of that damned thing, I'll do it myself."

"Get rid of it?" I thought, knowing how nice it would look parked on the tracks with our cabooses. As soon as I thought he'd recovered his composure, I went into his office to see him about it. By then he was no longer quite so eager to make the rash disposal, but he did urge me to contact his boss about it.

We wrote to that individual, sending along a signed copy of our 320-page photo book on his territory, hoping that it would show him the seriousness of our request. He must have recognized it, for we soon got a message in our mailbox that the old three-wheeler was ours to go get. It was the last of its type seen anywhere on the railroad around here.

Speaking of velocipedes and such brings to mind this railroad thought provoker, an anonymous poem called ''The Section Foreman's Epitaph'':

> Here lies the body of William Jay,
>   Who died maintaining his right of way.
> He was right,—dead right—, as he sped along,
>   But he's just as dead as if he was wrong.

Now, getting back to laws about handcars: Connecticut will fine you if you leave one on a highway! Vermont will get you only if you leave it at a crossing. Although railroads use these vehicles less and less, there are many collectors of them who might take note of these laws! If fact, there's even a Motor Car Collectors Association, which periodically holds rolling meetings on trackage, for which various rail companies give them permission.

The most unusual event to happen aboard a motorized track car has to be the birth of the Beck twins of Saskatchewan, in 1940. Their father, a Canadian National trackman, was trying to rush the mother through heavy rain to the nearest hospital, thirty miles away. Instead, he became midwife, midway in nowhere, and soon the track car's crew increased from two to four. How many doctors at delivery time have had to look up and down the tracks to make sure the operating table wouldn't get hit by a train?

Idaho may seem a backwoods state to some, but they've always had smart trainmen! Laws do not allow them to work on trains unless they can read and write. And if that rule wasn't enough to remind new recruits of Ma and Pa back home, laws also caused them to be fined for not phoning when their train was late!

Mississippi trainmen have had to be pretty much on the ball, too. Putting a passenger in the wrong compartment could bring them a fine of $500. In New Mexico that kind of fine is also given a trainman who overcharges a passenger (and the passenger gets the money!).

Texas, apparently not wanting its trains to further its cowpoke image, passed laws that made them among the very cleanest in the world. All interurban cars had to be hosed down once a day and fumigated as soon as germs were found. (Imagine a Texan in a uniform saying he's the "germ inspector"!) Regular railroad coaches were to be disinfected every other day, though sleeping-car blankets were only cleaned every ninety days.

And how is this for the grand finale of railroad laws: "When two trains approach each other at a crossing, they shall both come to a full stop, and neither shall start up until the other has gone." What's your guess where that law comes from? The rule books of Amtrak or VIA? No, it's from Kansas, many years ago, though it makes you wonder, doesn't it?

The Red and the Green

A little child on a sick bed lay
    And to death seemed very near;
Her parents' pride, and the only child
    Of a railroad engineer,
His duty called him from those he loved,
    From his home where lights were dimmed.
While tears he shed, to his wife he said,
    I'll leave two lanterns trimmed."

Chorus
Just set a light when I pass tonight,
    Set it where it can be seen.

If our darling's dead, then show the red,
If she's better, show the green.

In that small house by the RR side,
  'Twas the mother's watchful eye,
Saw a gleam of hope in the feeble smile,
  As the train went rushing by,
Just one short look. 'Twas his only chance,
  But the signal light was seen.
On the midnight air there rose a prayer,
  "Thank God, the light is green!"

—Anonymous, 1943

The Moose
by My Caboose . . .
and Other Animal Tales

Kind of a dreary day this is, the third one of the new year (1987). Thick, snowy rain is coming down this afternoon, following several hours of a real snowstorm this morning. If it turns cold, next, as it surely will at this time of year in the Canadian Rockies, then our poor elk will have a heck of a time pawing through the frozen crust down to their main feed. They'll have to compete with the moose and deer for brush tips and higher browse.

I'm alone here this week, king of Caboose Camp, while the family is away to celebrate the New Year's holidays with relatives in the tribe. There's a big indoor Pow-Wow dance held each New Year's Eve by the Bloods of Alberta, a tradition they began after settling down on their reserve and adopting some of the "white man's" ways. In the Blackfoot language, they named this New Year's event the "Kissing Dance"; if you ever went to one at midnight, you'd know exactly why! Visitors from all over come to attend. We've been to this dance many times; I sure wanted to go again this year. My fellow Magpie Society members were the sponsors, and I wanted to help them. (Honest, that's *the* reason I was so eager to go!) Beverly and the kids went, but I had to settle for taped powwow music, with only the narrow corridor of my caboose to dance in.

The dogs, in the darkness outside, must have decided there was a scuffle going on—that someone had managed to sneak in past them. They started barking up a storm until I went out on the back platform and calmed them down. Soon afterward, I heard one of them again snoring contentedly beneath my floor. They like to sleep on piles of straw I put between the ties for their use.

When there's no one at the house, like now, the dogs end up spending most of their time around here. Even so, I woke up this morning to the unmistakably heavy crunching of elks' feet, right outside. There are a couple of grassy patches nearby that they really like, so their tracks are generally visible in the snow around here; it is not unusual for me to climb up into the cupola on an early morning and watch a few of them grazing right down below. Our dogs learned from us when they were very young that their interference is not allowed. Sometimes they sit up and watch in excited silence, their bodies trembling from having these big wild animals less than three or four leaps away. After a while they relax again, often going back to sleep.

THE RABBIT WHOSE HOME WAS A CABOOSE

Having animals around a retired caboose like mine seems only natural, so to speak. Sometimes the dogs even climb the steps and come inside for a visit, though they generally live outdoors. The kids also bring in their cats, while chickadees and jays eat fat and crumbs I put out for them. Beautiful humming-birds fly around here almost daily in the summertime, their dazzling colors often shining in through my windows. Perhaps they are attracted by the red color painted on the walls and other places.

Back in the era of steam, one CP conductor had a pet that actually rode around in a working caboose with him. It traveled up and down tracks in southern Ontario aboard a wayfreight that worked between the cities of London and Windsor. This pet was a rabbit, perhaps the only one that ever lived in a caboose.

Conductor A. R. McDonald adopted the bunny as a wild baby after it was nearly run over while standing on the tracks. Naming it Sandy, McDonald cared for this long-eared crew member over the next four years, during which he figured they rode at least 100,000 miles together. He had originally intended to turn it loose as soon as it was grown. But by then it was apparently so fond of railway life that when the train started to roll away, it followed alongside, until the conductor finally stopped the train and took it back in.

Sandy's favorite spot in the caboose was right on top of the conductor's desk. The rabbit learned to recognize the short whistle blasts that indicated the train was about to start. Upon hearing them, he would stiffen up and raise his long ears straight up in preparation for the upcoming jolt. Since the caboose was also a rolling home for McDonald and his men, it was not switched so often nor so roughly as ordinary freight cars.

The rabbit became very devoted to McDonald, who fed it a basic diet of grass and leaves, plus bananas, fruit cake and cookies from his lunchbox. He even got Sandy housebroken, providing him with a box of sand for the purpose.

RAILDOGS

Moving beyond caboose pets to the general theme of railroads and animals, the number of available anecdotes increases tremendously. Canines account for the greatest number, since so-called "railroad dogs" existed continually around stations and roundhouses from coast to coast.

Old Shep of Fort Benton

Surely one of the saddest stories of rail dogs must be that of Old Shep of Fort Benton, Montana. The story comes from Ed Shields, a Great Northern conductor who retired and took his caboose home with him. A year later, incidentally, he was elected mayor of Great Falls, becoming the first known such official to use a caboose for part of his duties.

Ed said that Shep's master was a sheepherder who died out

on the Montana prairie in the 1930s. The faithful dog followed when the body was brought to Fort Benton, watching as it was loaded on an express train at the station, to be shipped for burial elsewhere. The poor dog watched the train pull out, somehow getting the idea that another would bring his master back. From then on, he eagerly greeted every arriving train, keeping to himself underneath the station at all other times.

At first he refused all offers of food and friendship; railroad men who saw him figured he would soon die. But five years later, he was still healthy, having settled in and accepted regular handouts from train crews, section men and the station agent. Even dining-car chefs saved choice tidbits to give him on their way through. Until his final days, he never failed to meet them at train time.

The Mascot and Other Faithful Dogs

So many dogs have been mascots around railroads that one could conceivably write a full volume about their stories and pedigrees. For instance:

Rags was the little fox terrier mascot of switching crews in Chicago & North Western's Dearborn Street yard in Chicago, riding engines and cabooses, besides hanging out in crew shacks and the like. Everyone liked this dog and contributed to its well-being. Although blind in one eye, this little mascot gained headline fame one day in the 1930s for saving a man's life.

Riding in the cab of a switcher one night, Rags suddenly jumped from the open window, seven feet down to the ground, then ran ahead barking excitedly. The engineer stopped his switcher, and a crewman went down to investigate. He found Rags barking at an unconscious man stretched across the tracks, not far ahead of the engine.

For this deed, Rags was honored by the Anti-Cruelty Society, then exhibited at the Skokie Valley Kennel Club Show in Chicago. On his collar Rags carried a tag which simply read, "If lost, return to C&NW Ry., 313 N. Dearborn St., Chicago."

The Boston & Maine employees magazine told about a train crew that saved a pup from drowning. They were switching cars one winter day at Haverhill, Massachusetts, along the Little River, when switchman Joseph Baker noticed an animal had broken through the thin ice on the river. Baker signaled for the engineer to stop.

The entire crew rushed to the river bank, the fireman bringing his long clinker hook. With it he was able to drag the nearly frozen pup out of the water. A coat and the warmth of the locomotive cab soon revived the shivering animal, letting the men get back to their work.

And how's this for a faithful pet: A mutt named Jack followed his owner to the Chicago, Burlington & Quincy station in Hannibal, Missouri, some time during the early parts of World War II, not knowing his owner was headed for army service. Seeing his master board the train, he refused to leave the station afterward, rushing up to check passengers every time a train pulled in. Faith paid off, as the owner eventually came home on a furlough, finding old Jack still waiting on the platform.

A sadder version of such a tale begins one morning back in 1917, when a group of young army recruits boarded a Southern Pacific train at the station in Albany, Oregon, bound for World War I and France. Letters came from overseas . . . eventually a telegram to Henry White, father of one of the boys, bringing official government word: "Killed in action."

The poor father couldn't believe it: His happy, healthy son was hardly grown up; there must have been a mistake. When soldiers started returning from France, Henry White was down at the station, meeting every train, looking eagerly into each new crowd for his boy. Train after train arrived. Eventually everyone was back, but Henry White still waited for his son. The war was long over, but he kept on waiting. His pathetic figure became a fixture on the station platform. He met even the night trains, never giving up hope, often helping some elderly person or single mother with children. Nearly twenty years passed, until finally Henry White didn't show up anymore. When they found him dead in his lonely room, someone said he had gotten tired of waiting for his son and had gone to look for him.

ROUNDHOUSE CATS

Here's a tearjerker about a roundhouse cat and her kittens. While the pussy kept mice from the engine stalls and turntable area in CN's Calgary yard, she got herself pregnant and soon had kittens to feed. Perhaps the grub ran out and she decided to seek new lodging, or else a cold night was coming up and she thought the kittens needed a warmer place. At any rate, the family made itself at home in a casting between the front wheels of a passenger-hauling oil-electric car No. 15872. In that place, they made a fairly speedy trip of 247 miles to Edmonton, apparently arriving there safely.

Mama cat must have gone out scouting for food and perhaps a new home; she missed the train departure, and the kittens could not alert the conductor. Waiting faithfully around the station for a day and a half, poor Mama was dealt a sad blow when the train came back to Edmonton—her litter was still between the wheels, but either starved or frozen to death. She accompanied them back to Calgary in the same place, no doubt mourning the whole 247 miles. Back in the roundhouse, she took them down one at a time, and when the workers saw her they buried them just outside.

Because dogs became more intimate with humans than cats, the latter have not been mentioned as often in railroad folklore as the former. However, the *Canadian National Magazine* of June 1943 featured Mickey, a very active rail cat in Winnipeg, Manitoba. Said the story:

> Every railway building of importance on the system has its cat, [mainly because society has] failed completely to invent a better mouse-trap. . . . Some of these cats are officially on the payroll for board and lodging. Most, however, subsist by their skill and agility as mice catchers and upon the charity of the railway workers. . . .

The most shamelessly wanton feline is a resident of Winnipeg . . . named "Mickey." According to Charles Patton, commissary storekeeper who, for the past nine years, has been fated to occupy the same premises as "Mickey," her amorous adventures have added at least 125 kittens to the animal kingdom.

For an expenditure of a few cents per day for milk, "Mickey" has saved the company thousands of dollars from damage by mice.

Mickey and her 125 offspring had a distant rival in Boots, a tan and tiger-striped cat said to have raised 150 kittens in a desk drawer of John Betts, Boston & Maine yardmaster at White River Junction, Maine. The B&M employees magazine said Boots was known to all railroaders passing through the junction, after her arrival some eight years earlier aboard an empty boxcar, just like a hobo. She apparently liked boxcars and entered them regularly to catch mice. One time she got a free trip to Berlin, New Hampshire, that way—by accident, of course—but a brakeman there recognized her and promptly sent her back.

Boots had not only a cat's proverbial nine lives, but also a total of thirty-two toes, a distinction carried by all her offspring. A passing snowplow once buried her under a pile of snow and ice for six days before she was discovered. Another time she failed the clear the main line in time for a passenger train, which clipped off part of her tail. She was kept well fed by the yardmaster and many other employees, several of whom had taken home her kittens as family pets. There must yet be many descendants of Boots in that part of Maine, perhaps recognizable by their thirty-two toes and a peculiar interest in passing trains.

At the Mountain Street depot of the Canadian National Express in Montreal there dwelled a cat named Jenny. She resided in luxurious splendor, spoiled by the boys, who tossed her delicacies from their lunch boxes.

The CN Express department in Vancouver, British Columbia, had a cat named Fanny that liked riding around on express wagons and platform trucks, though only when she knew the driver. She also learned to hang around dining cars of trains at the Vancouver station, from which she usually received handouts of food. One day Fanny turned up missing, so everyone on the railway kept their eyes open for the cat. Traffic supervisor Jack Perry finally found her—or thought he did—in Chilliwack, some miles away, but when he brought this cat to Vancouver the real Fanny had already returned. After that there was some speculation as to the background of the look-alike picked up by Jack.

PIG FUELS ENGINE

This isn't exactly a railroad pet story, but it involves a train and an animal, and the idea might be of use the next time there is an oil shortage—at least to rural tourist railroads caught short of fuel for their steam engines.

We're on the Ohio Central Railway, back in the late 1800s. Our switching crew has engine No. 17, a little four-wheeled goat with a diamond stack and a hard time pulling twelve loaded ore cars from the yard up to the dock.

During this night of switching, we're down at the Lake Shore stockyards to move some cars of hogs. On the trackside platform lies one of the porkers, "deader 'n a doornail."

"There's some good fuel," says Conductor Hennessy to Jack Balfe, our engineer, who nods his head. Fireman Westcott says that would make the old teakettle heat up all right. Thus, taking his cue, the conductor gets us together to drag the beast into the cab. After we finish switching the stockyards, we've got a couple of dozen loads of ore to haul up to the dock, and that's when we need the old girl steaming.

Now we're coupled up to the first twelve cars and the fireman's got a good fire blazing. Together we push and struggle to squeeze that 200-pound hog through the firebox door. Luckily, it's pretty big, since this here's a woodburner. My, listen to that sizzling and popping down inside there! Look at the gauge starting to climb. We'd better get rolling to use up some of that steam, before the boiler blows wide open!

From there on we're flying up and down the climb to the docks, as if we had a mainline engine with ten drivers, instead of our tiny four. Even at the top of the grade, the safety pops are still open, with steam shooting thirty feet up into the air. The dockworkers are looking down at us with their mouths hanging open. It must have been like seeing a Shetland pony trotting around lively with a loaded beer wagon. For years after, when an engine on the line refused to work well, someone would say, "Get her some pork!"

FRESH MEAT

Turkey for Thanksgiving

Engineers of speeding express trains must have occasionally gotten birds and other things in through their cab windows, though probably none as big as that hog. The prize event of this sort happened down south on the Seaboard Air Line when an engineer named Yates ended up with Thanksgiving dinner for his family, after a big wild turkey lost a battle with his machine, back in 1929.

Meat

Back when refrigerator cars were kept cold with big chunks of ice instead of with motors, one of them fell over sideways on the old Iron Mountain Railroad, down in Alexandria, Louisiana. It had been standing still, parked on a track up on a sunny hill. There was no wind and the nearest person was some distance away. How could it have toppled over?

The car had been full of fresh meats, hanging on hooks from the ceiling of the car. As the ice melted and shifted to the cooler side of the car, the swinging meat leaned over with it until finally the whole car followed.

Another car of fresh meat left the tracks of the Rock Island Line in much more mysterious circumstances, back in the winter of 1927. Traveling rapidly downgrade on a hotshot freight, the meat car lost a piece of its rigging, which fell under the rear wheels and caused them to jump the track. At the moment of derailment, the car was at such an angle that the couplers at both ends came apart from their mates of the facing cars, one slipping up, the other down. In the next instant, the derailed wheels turned sharply outward in such a way as to make the car fall on its side completely parallel with the train, after which it slid down a deep embankment.

Now, of course, the air hoses came apart, and the train's brake system went into emergency, but that was not an unusual occurrence in those days. Somehow, none of the other cars derailed in the process. When the trainmen found that two cars were uncoupled, they assumed this was the cause of the airline break, so they coupled their train back together and proceeded to their destination without further incident. The missing car was discovered soon afterward by passing section men.

FOUR-FOOTED FRIENDS AND ENEMIES

Cow Derails Train, Gets Eaten

Here's the story of a branch-line mixed train whose passengers and crew got an unexpected dividend as the result of a collision that derailed their engine.

Leaving the prairie town of Lethbridge, Alberta, one afternoon in the winter of 1915, this train soon encountered a blizzard that left its engineer with virtually no visibility. Practically "running blind," as they say in these cases, he wasn't ten miles out of town when his engine struck a bunch of cattle that had congregated on the tracks.

Although the engine was immediately derailed, its speed was so slow that there was little damage and no injuries. Unfortunately, the storm had broken the telegraph wire, so the train's conductor was unable to send word of their plight back to Lethbridge. It was considered too dangerous for anyone to try walking back, so they settled down for a long wait, knowing there would be another train on the line eventually.

The crowd of ten or twelve people, including the five-man crew, got along well and stayed warm, but stomachs grumbled louder and louder as day turned into evening.

The locomotive fireman took matters into his own hands, so to speak, going out to one of the dead cows and cutting from it a sizeable chunk with his pocket knife. After roasting this meat on the end of his clinker bar, held carefully over the banked coals in the locomotive's firebox, he surprised everyone in the warm coach with a fresh, hot roast. Good thing the food was so near at hand, since it was two days before the blizzard let up enough for plows to come and dig the stranded train out. By that time, the cow had grown considerably smaller.

Moose Holds Up Train, Ends Up on Dinner Table

The Alaska Railroad is a modern line that usually operates on a regular schedule. In Alaska, like anywhere, nature sometimes throws things on the railroad off balance. Not infrequently the perpetrator is a wild animal, such as the moose in this story.

A plow train was clearing the Alaska Railroad's tracks about 150 miles north of Anchorage, one time, when this moose was discovered to be in the path. Actually, he'd been discovered some while earlier by the crew of a freight train that originally started out far in advance of the plow. The moose was wandering down the tracks, either unable or unwilling to climb up the tall banks of snow from earlier plowings which paralleled the right of way.

Unable to get the moose out of the way, the freight followed slowly behind. The plow train, when it caught up, had no choice but to join the parade, and after a while, a couple more freight trains joined further behind. Imagine this moose leading four trains over their own line!

At a small bridge, the moose found enough room to step aside, letting the original freight pass by. As soon as it was gone, however, he stepped back on the tracks and continued his journey, now with the plow train right behind. The plow operator had less patience than the freight train crew, signaling for the locomotive engineer to run closer and closer behind the moose. This finally angered the animal, so he turned around, lowered his antlers and prepared to fight. All the trains in his wake ground to a halt.

The crew tried its locomotive's whistle and bell, then snowballs and angry words, but the moose refused to budge. Eventually one crew member was able to get past the animal and walk to a section house with a phone, from which a message for help was sent out. A rifle was brought, along with special permission from the Game Commission to shoot it. That night a number of train crews had a good supper whose main ingredient left behind memories for a long time after.

Elephants Get Freight Train Up Pass

Here's an interesting way of powering trains over the mountains—used not in the Himalayas, but in the Colorado Rockies—with an engine in front and two elephants in back! Back around 1900 Barnum and Bailey hired the narrow-gauge Denver, South Park & Pacific Railroad to haul part of its circus from Denver out to some of the smaller mining towns along its line in Colorado. Three boxcars and a coach carried the whole "big top," including two elephants. But near the mountain summit the locomotive just couldn't handle the load any more—even with only four cars. Removing the elephants, which weighed three tons each, not only lessened the load tremendously (the engine weighed little more than the two of them!), but also the elephants were found willing to push with their heads from behind. (I hope the engineer had enough brakes for the other side. Picture two elephants on top of the Rockies waving their train goodbye!)

Mule Derails Passenger Train

Railroad officials generally figure most derailments are the cause of some jackass, although the power of rail unions forces them to keep these opinions private. But this train, near McAlester, Oklahoma, in 1912, really was derailed by such a four-legged beast. Engine No. 368 was leading a southbound train on the Missouri-Kansas-Texas Railroad, better known as the Katy, when it hit a small herd of mules grazing by the track. One of them was hurled ahead into a switchstand, which broke from the impact, causing the switch to be relined for a coal spur. Many passengers were killed and injured in the resulting collision between their speeding train and the parked coal cars.

Horse Kicks Train

Everybody knows it's not safe to walk too close behind a horse, but this engineer didn't think the rule applied to his train as well.

It seems that a bunch of horses got out of a stock car left on a siding between Moncton, New Brunswick, and Truro, Nova Scotia, sometime during the "Dirty Thirties." Along came the Canadian National's crack passenger train, the *Ocean Limited,* passing on the adjacent main line.

That train must have been moving along pretty slowly, since the offended horse not only kicked it, but managed also to break the train line that controlled the air brakes. This made the *Ocean Limited* come to a sudden halt, with several passengers probably calling the engineer names dealing with the hindward portion of a horse's anatomy, not realizing how close they actually were to the true cause of their unexpected discomfort. The train's journey to Halifax did not continue until someone found the broken train line and made emergency repairs.

Train-Riding Steer Snags a Lamp

The Regina *Leader Post* reported the following incident from along the Canadian Pacific main line in the early 1940s. Among those riding a CP Rail freight train from Mankota to Moose Jaw, Saskatchewan, was a western steer whose horns were so long that they protruded two or three feet from between the boards of its stock car.

Soon after this train left Mankota, section foreman Jim Gardner wondered what became of a lamp he had earlier lit and placed atop its mainline switch stand. The answer came to him after some hours, in a telegram from Moose Jaw. The lamp had been found upon the freight train's arrival there, still hanging from one of the steer's long horns!

A BIRD'S NEST ON AN ENGINE

Old Indian stories occasionally tell of hunters who found birds' nests hidden in the thick hair between the horns of buffaloes they had shot. Perhaps a certain robin in Peterborough, Ontario, was the descendant of such daring egg-layers, since she chose to build her nest aboard an active steam locomotive, long after the buffalo days, during the spring of 1940.

CPR engineer F. White said it all started when a pair of robins began building their nest underneath the running board of his engine, No. 840, the Peterborough yard switcher. They must have liked the engine's warmth, since their little homesite was just a few inches from the side of the firebox.

At first, the switching crew paid little attention to the birds, figuring they would soon give up their unusual attempt. But after a couple of days the nest was actually finished! Soon after that it was found to contain three little blue eggs.

Now the story began to receive public attention, and bird experts came to see the nest firsthand. Although the birds continued with their household efforts, everyone said they would eventually give up. Meanwhile, the engine continued with its daily yard work, going up and down the tracks and making the usual kinds of racket.

Among traditions held in high esteem by railway men is that of home and family, even if only that of little birds. As a result, the switching crew made a special effort to do its work as gently as possible, though even that was a far cry from the usual conditions in maternity wards. The mother robin, for her part, must have realized that she was among friends, since she refused to abandon her efforts. Every time the engine started to move, she flew up and around, until it came to a stop again, at which point she would sit back down on her eggs. It was reported that she had peace in her household only at nights and on Sundays.

Finally, one morning a little bird was hatched, and the following day came two more, making a perfect record. The engine crew had a celebration for this historic feat, although their joy was short-lived. The next day they learned that their engine was due for an overhaul in the roundhouse. Thinking that the faithful mother robin would never survive the change of atmosphere, they decided to remove the nest for her own safety. Thus they built a little box on one of the yard's lampposts, and moved the nest with its young occupants into it.

But when the mother robin refused to enter their box, the crew had to move it back down near its original spot on the engine. When she finally got used to this change, they moved the box to the top of a pole once again, and this time the mother accepted the change, so that her engine could be sent into the roundhouse.

By the time work was completed on the engine, the baby robins were already learning to fly. Then the crew wished they had at least put bands on the legs of their "adopted children," so that they could watch for them in following seasons to see if they'd come back to the yard again.

THE ANT

How about an ant stopping a freight train? Picture the little critter acting like the straw that broke the camel's back. How? Getting pulverized and thus greasing up the rails? No, this one must have been trained for intelligence operations, because he wasn't even on the tracks when the holdup occurred; he was deep inside the intricate machinery.

It was September 1930, on the Southern, near Bearden, Tennessee. Train No. 41 had been stopped by a red signal on the main line, though it was supposed to have rights over all others. It took some time to discover a small object that was keeping the relay contacts of the "clear" signal indicator from joining. Closer inspection showed this to be a large red ant, which had apparently been crushed when the signal attempted to show clear.

NICK MORANT'S ANIMAL STORIES

The following animal tales come from CP Rail company photographer Nick Morant, long a resident of Banff National Park:

Snakes turn up in unexpected places along the right-of-way. There's an historic train order among collectors' files in the Medicine Hat area that warns crews: "Be on the alert for rattle-snakes around Empress yards."

In a conversation, Cliff Gunning, regional signals supervisor at Toronto, recalled snakes going into his equipment boxes to change their skins and leaving unoccupied "overcoats" hanging across relay boxes. He also explained that spiders building webs across signal lenses can considerably impair CP Rail's efficiency, and there have been occasions when insects, squashed between electrical contact points, have caused technical failures.

CP telecommunications people have had a measure of attention from flying creatures like the stubborn osprey [large hawk] that insisted on building her nest on a certain line pole at Banff, Alberta. Lineman George Scott fought a losing battle with the bird until telecommunications finally conceded and built an extra crossarm on the pole especially for the nesting bird. It remains there today, tribute to an osprey with a one-track mind.

Birds seem to have the ability to get into everyone's thatch. They build nests on drawbars of boxcars awaiting maintenance on shop tracks. These are tenderly moved, "tenants" intact, to a place of mutual convenience. Hawks attack linemen on the prairies. "Dayliners" in Alberta have bars on their front windows to protect enginemen from flying pheasants. A woodpecker near Sicamous, British Columbia, believed that the humming noise of a simple rectifier was created by insects in the wooden box and drilled holes in a fruitless search for a square meal.

There are countless tales of dogs. A character named "Boomer" turned up around Moose Jaw. He traveled all over the various divisions and branch lines with train crews for two years—riding engines, cabooses and baggage cars; leaving and returning unexpectedly in various towns and villages. Another was "Jiggs," who used to assist train crews in shunting operations near Drumheller, Alberta. He could jump on a moving engine as expertly as any crew member.

But undoubtedly the most outstanding canine was "Duke," who used to reign over the platform at Schreiber, Ontario, thirty years ago and whose guardian in those days was a famous one-armed CP constable, Jack Handel. Duke was an undisputed king and veteran railroader who always stayed nights at the YMCA with the rest of the boys. He was once involved in saving the lives of two youngsters caught in a raging blizzard. On another occasion, he drew the attention of a passing train crew to a man freezing to death along the tracks. For this, he was recognized by the Humane Society, taken to Toronto and awarded a medal. Duke used to await all passenger trains and posted himself always at the exact spot where dining cars stopped. He expected and received due homage from all chefs. Passengers and anyone else in the neighborhood were permitted to examine the citation on his collar, and he actually used to turn his head to the side a bit to make things easier for admirers.

The Winnipeg Investigation Department have record of a poodle that escaped custody of a baggageman at Fort Williams, Ontario. The animal was seen adventuring throughout the lakehead area, but no one could catch it and collect the offered reward. Friendly words fell on deaf ears. One day, however, a Quebecer happened along and called out, "Hey there, *viens ici, mon pitou!*" He then collared the canine and the reward. The poodle had come from a French family and didn't understand English. Proof that it pays to be bilingual!

A moose was once removed from the lower Spiral Tunnel in the Rockies by a sectionman, a quick-thinking fellow named Jim Dominicis, armed only with a lamp and an iron nerve. He also must have had a strong thumb and forefinger, for he led the animal out of the darkness by the ear. Should anyone be so foolish as to doubt this story, Jim's superior officer was one Andy Montalbetti . . . who will vouch for its authenticity. Not only that, but he'll cap the yarn by adding that, at about the time Jim discovered the animal, there was a train coming down the hill. The two, man and moose, stood back against the wall, in the manner approved by all tunnel workers, to let the train go by. Then led by the ear, moose accompanied man to the tunnel mouth, freedom and safety.

Moose, especially in the fall, have a worldwide reputation for suicidal truculence. They resent trains passing through their territory. Some years ago *The Canadian*, highballing west, encountered a large bull moose near Lake Louise. He refused to move from the track and the train was brought to a halt. A moose carcass underneath the low clearance of a diesel can cause mechanical ructions—so it is no humanitarian impulse that necessarily impels the engineer to come to a stop. The accepted practice for moose removal is to slowly and deliberately push him off the track by sheer locomotive power. So it was in this case and, having lost twenty minutes, the train was on its way again. A note was tossed to a section crew to go back and chase the animal away before arrival of the eastbound *Canadian*.

At the meet, the eastbound *Canadian*'s engineer, Harry Eisenstein, took a message from the other train, warning of the moose at a certain mileage and instructing to watch out for the section crew.

As the train approached the area, there was the section men's track motor beside the right-of-way, but no sign of its crew. At the next bend, there stood the moose in the middle of the track, belligerently facing westward. Once again *The Canadian* was stopped.

Ear-splitting blasts from the engine horn had no effect, so the bunting technique was again employed and the disgruntled animal found himself beside the track for the second time. Wes Cudney, one of the train crew, said to a mate: "Wonder where the sectionmen got to?"

A few seconds later, the mystery was solved. "There they were," recalled Wes, "all three of them—each one up in the wires of the telegraph pole of his choice. They were still hollering for help as Eisenstein opened up the throttle to make up the lost time."

The classic tale of confusion in a caboose is related by George Davis . . . then a conductor on freights between Field and Calgary in the days of steam and before two-way radios. You're invited to bear with George's story.

A forty-car freight, drawn by a 5900 locomotive, eastbound at Lake Louise, was handed orders for a "meet" with three other trains at Castle Mountain siding. The side-trackings, George thought, would give him and his brakeman a wonderful opportunity to make themselves a hot breakfast.

As soon as they were in the siding and the switch safely locked, out came the bacon, the eggs and all the accompanying goodies that were such a feature of caboose life. Soon the surrounding atmosphere was filled with inviting aromas.

Seated at the table and just about to dig into the frypan, the two men felt a movement of the caboose—an effect that always heralds the arrival of a visitor as he swings onto the step. George and his companion expected to see the section foreman or another "brakie," Fred Ramsey, dropping in for a coffee. Instead, there loomed in the doorway a large black bear accompanied by two cubs.

Hoping to get the bears off the van, George tried to toss a piece of bread out the doorway but, unfortunately, it struck the wall and bounced back inside. In no time at all, that caboose became over-crowded.

The boys took to a built-in escape route—up the ladder into the cupola and out the window onto the roof. From down below, sounds of animal confusion arose—glass being shattered to the accompaniment of growling noises. A glance through the window showed the bears eating the prepared breakfast—one actually sitting in George's chair!

The "meet" completed, the engineer on George's train whistled off and moved into the main line with the three bears still holding their ground in the caboose. Brakeman Pawluck, wielding a bamboo rod, was finally able to dislodge the unwelcome guests at a siding at Massive, Alberta.

Van 436432 was a wreck: Lamps torn from their wall moorings; broken crockery everywhere; mattresses ripped open; and there remained a pungent reminder that three bears had passed that way.

Of all the animal anecdotes, I like best one about the man who boarded *The Canadian* at Calgary and slept in a hammock in the baggage car, all the way to Toronto. Unusual enough—but wait. His bedfellow was a young orangutang, and baggagemen related to me that it was quite a sight to see the two of them asleep in one another's arms in the swaying hammock—for all the world like an illustration from a jungle book for children.

CHAPTER EIGHT

Railroad Avenue and Depot Street

On a dark stormy night, as the train rolled along
    All the passengers had gone to bed
Except a young man with a babe in his arms
    Who sat with a bowed down head.
The innocent one began crying just then,
    As though its poor heart would break;
One angry man cried: "Make that kid stop its noise;
    It's keeping all of us awake!"
"Put it out," cried another. "Don't keep it in here.
    We've paid for our berth and want rest."
"Where is its mother? Go take it to her,"
    One lady quietly said.
"I wish that I could," was the man's sad reply,
    "But she's dead in the car ahead."

Chorus

While the train went rolling onward, a husband sat in tears,
Thinking of the happiness of just a few short years.
Baby's face brings pictures of a cherished hope that's fled,
For baby's cries can't waken her in the baggage car ahead.

Every eye filled with tears, as his story he told,
    Of a wife that was faithful and true,
Of how they had saved all their earnings for years
    Just to build up a home for two;
When heaven had sent them this sweet little babe,
    Their happy lives were blessed—
His heart seemed to break, when he mentioned her name,
    And in tears tried to tell them the rest.
The women arose to assist with the child,
    There were mothers and wives on that train,
And soon was the little one sleeping in peace,
    With no thought of sorrow or pain.
Next morn at the station, he bade them good-bye,
    "God bless you," he softly said.
They all had a story to tell in their homes,
    Of the baggage car ahead.

             —ANONYMOUS RAILROAD WORKER

Trackside facts and lore have made popular reading ever since the 1820s, when the first trains ran in North America. If you were to stay aboard this caboose for a time, you would become pretty familiar with railroad facts and lore, just by reading through some of the old railroad books and magazines that have accumulated in my closets. Many of you would be surprised by the great wealth of railroad material that has been printed—stories, photos, statistics and more. Anyone could find things of interest among this rail literature, even those who might not ordinarily pay much attention to trains.

Some of the following pages are from notes taken while perusing this rail literature. Greatest pleasure of this sort comes to us from a collection of *Railroad Magazine* that dates back to 1932. The boys and I obtained most of these from a friendly retired fellow over on the Alberta prairies, who sent the collection, saying they should be in our cabooses.

Despite its technological-sounding name, *Railroad Magazine* was more than just a periodical about trains; it was an institution. Starting in 1906, it served as an international meeting center for railroaders with creative minds. Among them were fiction writers, fact collectors, interviewers and lots of guys who just liked sharing stories. Among its thousands of readers, it was often hard to tell the railroad workers from the railfans, since many of them were both. In our own travels we have met several highly placed rail officials who have confessed to having first gotten involved with railroads as a hobby. Most of them were readers of *Railroad Magazine*, as well. Too busy now to practice their hobby, some of these men respond very favorably when approached with creative projects such as taking photographs or running excursion trains.

Railroad Magazine has a particularly fond place in our hearts because two of the boys and I once paid a memorable visit to its long-time editor, a singular old gentleman named Freeman Hubbard. He'd been with the magazine since the early thirties; we met him in 1977. Most of the time, his job had been a one-man show, with others contributing bits and pieces. A picture I took shows him with the boys in his cluttered office, upstairs on New York's Forty-second Street, just around the corner from Grand Central Station. You can imagine why my two young Rocky Mountaineers (they were then eight and four) will forever associate Freeman and his magazine with the greatest of train stations. Besides just wanting to meet this renowned editor of written railroad life, I had wanted to pay him tribute for the guidance he gave me at the start of my writing career.

I was fifteen when I brashly sent him four typed pages and some photos of a little California short line that was then still using a well-maintained steam engine each Tuesday of the week. He sent the piece right back and said that it bored him! Not only that, but he took the article apart, piece by piece, pointing out all its faults and weaknesses. At first I was crushed and insulted by this unwanted advice. What a start for a first article! But the lessons eventually got through to me, and since then they've grown and grown. How many newsstand-magazine editors do you know who would take the time to offer an unknown fifteen-year-old kid a brief correspondence course in creative writing?

Freeman didn't take much notice of the difference that I showed when I came to meet him, even when I said his influence had helped lead me to two contracts from New York book publishers. But I did see a kindly smile come out from under his gray mustache. When I mentioned that the books concerned Indian culture and lore instead of railroads, he chuckled and said that his wife was part Indian. Her father had been paymaster on early-day trains through the Oklahoma Indian Territory, her mother a woman from one of the tribes. I told him that my wife's grandfather had run an important stage stop on a wagon route through southern Alberta. His full-blooded Blackfoot wife had to learn to cook sausages and potatoes in an oven instead of roasting buffalo meat over open fires.

We were lucky to see Freeman when we did; not long afterward, *Railroad Magazine* was shut down and Freeman retired. To many, this signaled the end of a great era in railway life and lore. Two years later he passed away, at age eighty-seven.

Railroad Avenue happens to be the title of the most popular among several books written by Freeman Hubbard. While working on this volume, he asked readers to send him the names of cities and towns that had railroad designations, figuring to list them all. But he soon was made cognizant of the lengthiness of such a project. One man wrote to say that a book published in 1908 listed the following: 240 places with a Railroad Street; 230 with a Railroad Avenue; 13 with a Railroad Place; 8 with a Railroad Alley; 3 with a Railroad Circle and 2 with a Railroad Row. Among other railroad-related names, there were 96 places boasting a Depot Street; 17 with a Station Street; 2 with a Track Street and 10 with a Depot Square. Also on the list were a Locomotive Street, an Engineer Street and a Roundhouse Alley.

Our family is thinking to petition the city council of nearby Skookumchuck (population: forty-seven) to name a bridle path heading out our way "Caboose Boulevard."

TRACKSIDE TALES

Live Man Rides Train Home in Coffin

Chang Tsung-Chang was the proud governor and warlord of some thirty million people in Shantung Province, China. During a rebellion in 1928, he vowed to wipe out the insurgents or else be brought back home in a coffin. Defeated in battle but still alive, he kept his promise by riding home inside a red lacquered coffin aboard a flat car of the Chinese Eastern Railway. At six feet eight inches, he must have made an imposing sight, sitting up in his coffin and smoking a cigar, while behind him were private cars containing his harem of thirty wives.

On his return, Chang was driven into exile. A few years later he came back and tried to reclaim power, but was assassinated at the Tsinanfu railway station.

Expensive Trestle

How's this for a railroad bridge putting a dent into the local ecology. Back in 1852, when the Erie Railroad needed to span the Genesee River at Portageville, New York, its crews built what was then the world's largest wooden bridge—800 feet long, 200 feet high—by clearing more than 246 acres just to get the required timber.

A big celebration followed the first crossing of this huge bridge, though less than twenty-five years passed before the structure burnt to the ground. Another bridge was built in its place, and that one lasted well into the 1930s.

Riding the Iron Horse

Tosh Boyd didn't know what kind of wild ride he was in for one rainy night in the early 1930s, as he got into the saddle of his horse. Leaving his home at Harold, Kentucky, Tosh crossed nearby railroad tracks right in the path of a Chesapeake & Ohio freight train. His horse was killed, but somehow Tosh ended up on the locomotive pilot, still clinging to his saddle. Unnoticed by the busy crew, he rode twelve miles through the state, in this way, until the train arrived in Pikeville, where he got off unhurt.

Traveling Twins

Years ago, the Northern Pacific Railroad had a pair of passengers that they decided to treat as a single one. Daisy and Violet Hilton were famous Siamese twins in their time. NP auditor E. J. Johnson put out a bulletin to the line's conductors saying that, even though the twins occupied two seats, they should be charged for only one. "They are so joined together," he explained "that wherever one goes, the other must go; when one dies, the other must die; therefore one fare is valid."

Twins of a different sort who traveled trains a lot were Francis M. and Columbus E. Enslen, born on a farm near Elida, Ohio, on May 23, 1861. Both were engineers for thirty-eight years on the Pennsylvania Railroad, which must be some kind of record. Both were retired by the end of 1932, when they settled near each other in Fort Wayne, Indiana. But the railroad twins had one peculiar difference in life: Columbus married and fathered several children, while his brother always remained single.

Right of Way

Streetcar motormen had a frustrating rule to cope with in Bridgeport, Connecticut, during the early years of the twentieth century. A city ordinance allowed drivers of delivery trucks and wagons to park on streetcar tracks for five minutes. Some of these men were so competition-minded that they stood with watch in hand, waiting for the final seconds, before moving out of the way of stopped streetcars. One motorman found his route blocked by a wagon delivering pies, so he got out and helped himself to one, sitting down to enjoy it better. "What in hell are you doing," shouted the irate driver, coming out on the street from his delivery. "I'm eating a pie," replied the motorman calmly, "and if I'm stuck here much longer, I'll eat another one!" At that, the wagon was quickly moved.

How about the lucky hobo who fell from the freight train he was riding and got nothing worse than one leg cut off? Not so good, you say? Three cars passed over the leg before the conductor got his train stopped, rushing down to help the poor 'bo. The fellow thanked him for the help and said what he needed most was a sturdy stick, at least until such time as he could get himself another wooden leg!

Another guy with a wooden leg was Mose Cook, sort of a night watchman of engines on the Southern, down in Georgia.

After his leg broke accidentally on the job, his personal injury report became the first on any railroad to suggest shop repairs rather than a trip to the doctor!

Collisions

Early-day movies often featured car and train encounters; usually the participants remained uninjured, while around them everything was laid to waste. Apparently such incidents could happen in real life, too. Take this instance: Down in Atlanta, many years ago, two prosperous individuals were driving along North Avenue in a large touring car. While crossing several tracks, they suddenly found themselves in front of a fast-moving locomotive. In the resulting collision, their auto was totally demolished and a dog sitting between them was instantly killed, yet neither of them was even injured!

On November 16, 1931, a Reading freight train hit a wagon at a crossing in Pleasantville, New Jersey. Nothing unusual about that; it happened somewhere every day. The wagon disappeared into kindling under the train, but the impact unhitched the horse and knocked it to safety, at the same time depositing the driver, also safely, some hundred yards further up the track, where he passed out from having too much to drink!

Of course, we could fill several books with stories about road-crossing accidents that did not turn out so well. Railroaders have an old saying, "There's one time and place automobiles and trucks don't put trains out of business, and that's when they meet at the crossings."

Collisions between airplanes and trains are certainly much less common than between other types of vehicles, but they have been known to happen. In September 1931, a light plane crashed on the Southern's main line in South Carolina, badly injuring both pilot and passenger. The weather must have been bad, for shortly afterward the railroad's crack *Piedmont Limited* rushed by, knocking the disabled plane off the train tracks, yet kept right on going, its engineer having seen nothing to make him stop.

Car Hits Top of Train

It could only happen in New York! That's what they say, and it sure fits this dramatic episode. The year was 1938; William D. Lorenzo was taking his girlfriend out for a drive. They were crossing a bridge just as a New York Central train rolled by below. Suddenly another car pulled into De Lorenzo's path, so he swerved to avoid a collision. His car skidded and crashed through the bridge's guard rail, landing squarely on top of the moving train, with neither of the couple hurt! Now, as I was saying about your beautiful brown eyes, honey . . .

Plane Hits Train

A U.S. Army bomber on a World War II training flight, on August 8, 1943, crashed on tracks near Wendover, Utah, derailing a Western Pacific freight train whose crew didn't even see the plane. One flyer was killed and seven injured, but the train crew came away unhurt.

Train Rams Ship

Back around 1890, a switch engine was doing its work on the dock tracks of the Richmond, Fredericksburg & Potomac, at Richmond, Virginia, when its crew was suddenly showered by bits of broken wood. Within moments, deck hands of a freighter ship started a brawl, claiming the train crew had purposely rammed their vessel.

Apparently the ship's captain had docked his schooner so that its cargo of freight would be easy to unload, never noticing that the boat's jib boom stuck way across the tracks. Results of the fight were not recorded, but lawsuits from both sides were eventually settled by the courts in the railroad's favor.

Car Thieves

Thievery is not a subject we want to glorify in this book, yet it is hard not have a certain admiration for the gall of some. How about the fellows from an unnamed little southern town who waited until the crew of a local freight had gone to eat in a nearby restaurant before they went and removed a shiny Ford automobile being hauled inside a boxcar!

Believe It or Not

Newspaper headlines in 1931 told an amazing story involving the Great Northern's *Empire Builder*. Believe it or not, the whole train was picked up by a prairie cyclone and set back down a hundred feet from the tracks! Even more spooky was a story out of Kiowa, Kansas, in 1878, telling about a "waterspout" that enveloped a Santa Fe locomotive on an embankment and swept it away, crew and all, never to be seen again!

How about this for a crazy place to get off a train: Looney, Kentucky, on the Chesapeake & Ohio, once actually listed in that railroad's timetables.

In the 1940s the Erie Railroad had a company physician and surgeon named Dr. Matthew A. McGrail, who put in one day a week as locomotive fireman. He once operated on his own engineer, another time delivered a baby for his conductor's wife.

"It's railroadia psychasthenia," he was quoted to explain. "The symptoms are an avid and insatiable interest in all things railroading. Relief comes only from riding a locomotive once a week."

Did you know that railroad tracks running north and south are magnetized; those running in other directions are not? This magnetism is induced by the earth, itself, said to be a huge magnet. How about running real electric trains north and south that way, just like model railroads?

United States and Canada Hold Boundary Rail Record

An article in a 1936 issue of *Railway Age* pointed out that there were then fifty railroad crossings between the United States and Canada, which was far more than those of any other national boundary in the world. Between the United States and Mexico, at the same time, there were only eleven.

Million-Dollar Engineer's Cap

Who knows what kind of a hat George J. Kromer wore in 1897, when he first started working as a fireman for the Chicago & North Western? Like other fledgling employees in locomotive cabs, he no doubt looked forward to making his place on the right side, as locomotive engineer, though he surely didn't expect to make a permanent change in that job's image, affecting all North American engineers.

George lived in Kaukauna, Wisconsin, where the weather was so bad that others up and down the line nicknamed him "Stormy." During one particularly windy autumn, in 1905, "Stormy" Kromer went home to his wife, Ida, and asked her to sew him a cap that wouldn't blow off his head like the ones he'd been wearing. "A peaked sort of cap," he was supposed to have told her, "with a visor and an elastic sweatband."

Being a good seamstress, in addition to a faithful wife, Ida had the cap ready for her husband's next working day. He wore it and found it so comfortable that other members of his crew soon asked if Mrs. Kromer could make them similar ones. As word got around, she soon found herself with a busy and profitable sideline.

With money and encouragement from friends, the couple

eventually opened the Kromer Cap Company, employing some three dozen men and women in a small Milwaukee factory, where they sewed nothing but "Stormy" Kromer's "engineer's caps." At one point, orders reached well over 300,000 caps in a year, bringing the Kromers' revenues to over a million dollars and adding Stormy's name to railroad legend and folklore.

But the million-dollar business didn't satisfy "Stormy's" love of riding in engine cabs. Maintaining his seniority on the C&NW's Ashland division, he eventually became an engineer, leaving his successful, million-dollar hat business frequently in order to run a switch engine in the railroad's Kaukauna yard.

Man Overboard

We all have close calls with disaster as we go through our lives, but few of these would leave an imprint on our minds like this one, experienced by railway mail clerk A. L. Bemis, back in the summer of 1920.

Bemis was working on the Chicago, Burlington & Quincy, running on train No. 9 between Omaha and Denver. He was one of six men handling mail that night aboard the rolling post office. Of them, he had the toughest assignment: "station duty," which meant he had to take on and drop off mail at various stations along the way, even though the express train stopped at only a few of them.

It was Saturday night and the train was running late, largely because its stops at bigger cities were delayed by the loading of bulky Sunday papers. If you've seen a city paper shipping out its Sunday edition aboard trucks you have some idea of the large load crowding No. 9's mail car.

Switching mail bags at country stations "on the fly" was standard procedure, for which the railroads had made several improvements. First, the stretch of track where mail was to be dropped off had a specially graded portion that guided tumbling mail sacks (watch those fragile items!) away from the train's wheels. The clerk just had to make sure he pushed the sacks overboard at the right time, or there would be a lot of partial messages delivered the next day. (Crunch, now watch the wheels!)

Small-town mail was picked up by these speeding trains through a clever system whereby a sturdy sack was suspended from two ends on a post near the station. A long forked iron arm on the mail car "grabbed" this sack of mail and brought it along. After throwing off his sacks, Bemis then had to remove the snatched mail from the iron fork after each station, bringing it inside the mail car for sorting, being careful not to let it accidentally fall overboard.

No. 9 was about half an hour late leaving Lincoln, Nebraska, so the engineer tried to make up some lost time. Bemis got little chance to catch his breath, as one country station followed another. He got no help from fellow workers, who were kept busy sorting the contents of the various sacks and adding heavy newspapers to those about to be sealed and dropped off.

The next station on the nighttime route was a favorite for Bemis—the small town where he'd been born and raised. Still, he had little time to wonder about sleeping friends and neighbors as he got their mail ready to throw down. He figured the newspapers alone weighed probably 150 to 200 pounds.

To keep the mail sacks from scattering along the right-of-way, Bemis's final job each time was to tie them all together with stout cord, fastening a pouch with first class letters to the top. Approaching his hometown, he did this as usual, unaware that he had accidentally tied his strong brass key chain in with the cord. The chain was fastened to a reinforced buttonhole in his overalls!

Rumbling through the sleeping town, the train rapidly approached its station; Bemis knew every foot of the way by heart. One last curve, then he watched for a certain switchstand which was his marker for throwing the bags overboard. The instant he did that, he was yanked outside with the mail.

It so happened that there was no mail pickup at this town on weekends, so the forked iron arm on the mail car was empty. By instinct, Bemis grabbed this arm on his way out, clutching desperately as the heavy mail tugged fearfully at his body. Between the key chain and mail cord, there was enough length to allow the mail sacks to bounce along on the ground, each jerk threatening to tear the hapless clerk in half. If he was able to call for help, no one heard him amidst the sounds of the highballing train.

Main Street went by in a flash, as did the station platform and the depot itself. There was nothing anyone could have done, had they seen him dangling in the dark. He knew that, within moments, the mail bags would become entangled in switchstands at the far end of the yard, after which he would be thrown under the train or else bounced headfirst into the trackside gravel.

Suddenly he felt lightened, as the load dropped away and left him free. He managed to drag himself back in through the open baggage door, where he called out to his fellow workers. They came and stared in amazement, unable to do more than shake their heads and whistle.

There stood mail clerk Bemis, dressed in only one-half of his overalls! The weight of his load had torn them neatly down the front, right around the crotch and up the back; the whole left side had disappeared with the mail! A snapshot taken of him at that moment would surely have been a prize. The next station was a division point, where train crews were changed. Bemis managed to borrow some clothing before he went inside and phoned back to his hometown. The station operator there was an old boyhood friend. This fellow was on the verge of despair, having seen Bemis hanging in midair as the train roared by, and then managing to find only the mail sacks and parts of his torn clothing. He had not yet found time nor courage to report the affair and was immensely relieved to hear his friend's voice. The following day he met Bemis coming back on the next train and gave him back the sturdy chain, its keys still intact, plus the remains of the overalls.

Train Robber with a Black Bag

Train passengers are by and large an honest and trusting lot; they have to be, since they can't carry their luggage around with them when they go to the toilets, dining cars, or lounges. The following story is about a "black sheep"—a man who ironically dressed in dark suits and black hats while he traveled trains in search of robbery victims. It was told by Lawrence S. Howe, the railroad detective who tracked and finally arrested this crook.

It was in the early 1910s when detective Sergeant Howe was put on this case by his superior, the chief special agent of the Chicago, Rock Island & Pacific Railroad (better known as the Rock Island Line). Sketchy information regarding his quarry included the dark-dress description, the fact that all his crimes were carried out in the mid-West, and that he had a way of drugging his victims so that they knew little or nothing until afterward.

Howe compiled a list of the man's known crimes, plotting them on a map to determine if there was a pattern. Sure enough, Kansas City seemed to be at the center of a rough circle that contained the lines of several railroads that had been hit, including the Rock Island. Then, using police records, he began to trail likely suspects in that area, waiting to see further signs.

Aboard a Rock Island train headed for Chicago one day, the conductor came up to Howe and said he thought the wanted man was riding in the next coach ahead. A dark-dressed man in there had been acting suspiciously. Passenger train conductors were always on the lookout for odd behavior among their passengers, for whose welfare and safety they were, of course, responsible.

Detective Howe (a "gumshoe" in railroad talk) was accompanied by one of the railroad's regular policemen (called a "bull"). The two moved ahead to the next car, finding an empty pair of seats not far from the dark-dressed suspect, who appeared to be in friendly conversation with his younger, well-dressed neighbor. They saw him offer this neighbor a drink, poured from a bottle kept in a black bag that he carried with him. Soon the younger man was asleep, at which time the culprit picked his pockets, thinking himself unnoticed.

Before the two railroad employees could make their move, the suspect got up and went into a nearby toilet, carrying his black bag. Within moments he came back out, a finger on his right hand freshly bandaged. The two watchers waited to see what he was up to next.

Instead of returning to his seat beside the sleeping young victim, he moved one seat behind and sat down next to an elderly gentleman who was already asleep. He took out a newspaper, pretending to read, holding it so that his bandaged finger was near the old fellow's nose. About that time, the detective noticed the smell of chloroform in the air, from which he quickly surmised what was going on. The crook was about to pick the sleeping gentleman's pockets, but he wanted to make sure not to be caught in the act, so he intended to deepen his victim's sleep, as he had done to many others.

There was a quick scuffle, as detective and railroad bull got up and grabbed their suspect, who was not willing to give up easily. They managed to relieve him of a .45 caliber pistol, which he was trying to reach, then found also a .38 caliber, which he had just stolen from the younger sleeper. The black bag, tossed away during the struggle, was found to contain bandages, more chloroform, a bottle of liquor, plus crystal chloral like that which had been put into the young man's drink. The man was brought to trial in Davenport, Iowa, where he was sentenced to ten years in the penitentiary. However, three years later, Detective Howe saw him free again, paroled and working as a street cleaner in Des Moines.

Railroading Families

Firemen and conductors on the Western Maryland Railroad must have been puzzled numerous times during the 1940s and '50s wondering just which "Engineer Rhodes" they were working with. *Nine* brothers with that last name all held right-hand seats on WM locomotives, sharing among them 188 years of service. Crew dispatchers had to be careful to specify, when they called an Engineer Rhodes to handle a train, whether they wanted Bob, Burnell, Clint, Dale, Dick, Don, Paul, Preston or Sterling.

But there were no identity problems for the crew of the *Pennsylvania Limited,* especially when Conductor Harry A. Taylor made his final run on that train out of Fort Worth, Indiana, in 1950. Practically the whole gang—engineer, fireman, brakemen and so on—were his sons, six of them. Taylor had a seventh son, as well, but he was busy back in town, driving buses!

HOBO-ING IN AMERICA

Hoboes Ride Boxcar In and Out of Prison

Nelson L. Pinnell and his friend, Mark Creage, were taking a poor-man's journey through Colorado in 1907 when a boxcar they were on suddenly reached a much unwanted destination.

It was a hot summer afternoon when the two arrived in Canon City, having gotten a ride from a friendly crew aboard a lone locomotive changing home terminals. At Canon City they learned it would be well into the night before the next freight train was due to head out. Tired from traveling and looking for work, they went into the freight yard and found an empty boxcar in which to lie down and rest. The one they picked even had clean straw on the floor, so the two were soon dozing soundly.

A rude awakening came when something roughly coupled into their car. Before they could jump off, they were headed down the track at a good speed, pausing at the far end only long enough for the changing of a switch. Before they knew it, they found themselves down the line, so to speak, inside a penitentiary. Their car was apparently part of a train being delivered to that place. Hiding in a dark corner, the two penniless travelers expected to be caught momentarily by a guard, else to be found out later. They heard the engine uncouple and chuff away. But in a few moments, it came back, apparently performing switching maneuvers.

As sudden as their arrival, came their departure. Both men sighed with relief when their train passed out through the open, guarded gate. They got back to Canon City in time to catch the mainline freight heading out. They ended up finding jobs in Pueblo, Colorado, where Mark was hired by the Santa Fe Railroad as a brakeman, Nelson as a roundhouse worker. Later, Nelson also worked as locomotive inspector for the Southern Pacific. Neither of the two ever went to prison again.

A Letter From an Old Hobo

Fishbones wrote to say hello, and his letter came just as I reached the end of this chapter and wondered how to add something more about hoboes.

Well, he tells me that they're all getting together again this year around August 1 for their annual National Hobo Convention. The first time Fishbones wrote to us, some time back, he caught our attention by sending a coupon good for ''one bowl of mulligan stew,'' at such a convention.

His days of riding ''side-door Pullmans'' long over, old Fishbones has written a little book called *Hobo-ing in the 1930s*. He's well settled down now, out near Corinna, in the woods of Maine. There, he brews up a mean bug repellent called ''Irving's Fly Dope''; Irving Stevens is another of his ''handles.'' The ''fly dope'' comes free with a printed ''Anecdope,'' of which the following shall suffice as examples:

> Send Irving's Fly Dope to the store today!
> It sells well with the other goodies;
> All out of liquid and no more spray,
> Was all lapped up out in the woodies.

or,

Had truly intended to mow the lawn,
Borrowed Irving's Fly Dope from neighbor Pete;
Went fishing at the crack of dawn,
While grass grows longer under his feet.

Truly spoken like a retired hobo, I think.
Said Fishbones in his letter:

. . . I live three miles out in the country and often think of
owning a caboose and bulldoze down this 1830 farm house. The
north walls is caving in. The cellar freezes. And because of that
no sanitary system. It gets cool in "the library! . . ." There is
running water—I run after it to the well. . . .

This old farmhouse I call home is still better than sleeping
somewhere under a bridge. That squirrel under my bird feeder had
better beware it doesn't end up in a stew! On second thought, it
may be a reincarnated old hobo that couldn't make it South. Old
"Fishbones" will give it sunflower seeds and hopes this spring it
will go and "jungle" out in the woods. . . .

. . . And speaking of "jungles," this year will be my fifth
pilgrimage to Britt, Iowa, to attend the convention. The "jungle"
is located a block and a half from Britt's main street. A mile long
parade, topped off by mulligan stew and a coronation of king and
queen. A gala event where everyone is friendly, gathered around
a jungle camp fire each evening, singing railroad songs with va-
gabond guitar pickers. The SOO Railroad even bumps off a boxcar
for the bo's to sleep in! How about that for service! There is nothing
like a good warm boxcar and some cardboard for a bed!

Very few of the old hobos are left, as it was a strenuous life
. . . a spirit of adventure that led to new horizons. . . .

That old comradeship brings some of us back to Britt each
year. The reason for Britt being the spot for hobo conventions
goes back a long way. Not only are the mid-West farm people the
friendliest, but Iowa is in the middle of the annual harvest that starts
down in the Texas panhandle and ends up north in Saskatchewan
and Manitoba. The farmer depended on the hobo—"man with the
hoe [hoe boy]"—to help him thresh the wheat. For that reason the
mid-West folks were very tolerant of the travelling man that some-

times knocked on their back doors. More so than were the people of the east. . . .

I will say adios for now, as . . . this typewriter needs a rest. . . . May the great spirit be with you and to all God's children and birds and animals of the forest on these cold nights. I have never rode a caboose, but I have seen their lights twinkling going down the tracks. Consider me a friend of the cinder trail.

Sincerely,
Fishbones

THE "BOOMERS"

We met there 'neath a railroad bridge,
Did hobo Bill and I;
While java boiled in a tomato can,
And cinders got in our eye.

We talked of rails and better days;
And exchanged too many woes:
Of railroad bulls and right-of-ways;
Wondered why we were bo's.

Needing to explore "leaky tank" town;
Detoured there for the bumming;
Stemmed the drag up town and down:
The women saw us coming.

Beholding strangers in their midst,
Looked from behind the curtain cracks;
And tallied the supply of grits,
While dwelling near the railroad tracks.

We mooched too, stale bakery treats;
Scraped a butchers block for chops:
And after exploiting the streets,
Shied to the jungle like a fox.

Over the acrid smell of coal,
The chops fried in a battered pan:

Doing nothing for the soul,
They satisfied the inner man.

A scraggy dog crept into camp,
It was a scroungy feller;
And was considered a "loner" tramp
That hadn't heard of salmonella.

The music to the ears was sweet,
When a moving freight let whistle moan,
And shook the ground beneath our feet:
We tossed the hungry dog a bone.

Quaffed another pot of brew:
Journeyed a mile in others' shoes;
With never a care for the lot we drew,
We waited for changing of the crews.

We hearkened to a mournful sound
Coming from depths of a loyal beast;
As my friend caught a west bound,
And I grabbed the east.

—Irving L. Stevens (Fishbones), 1985.

"Come on back," says trainmaster John Egan, using standard railroad hand signal of a circular motion, as crews follow his guidance aboard two steam engines on New Hampshire's Conway Scenic Railroad. A special train was being made up as part of the tourist line's annual "Railfan Day" events. In real life John Egan is a conductor on the Grand Trunk, where he worked on the old caboose sitting here beside him, as well as on another one now used by he and his wife as a vacation home. AHW PHOTO

Above, "Caboose King" of America Don Denlinger welcomes the Canadian boy from the wild caboose. Behind them, symbolically, the U.S. flag flies over a caboose lettered CANADIAN PACIFIC. Taken on the roof of Don's office, store and entertainment center, this photo shows only part of his forty-unit Red Caboose Motel, which earned him notices by Ripley and in the *Guinness Book of World Records. Below,* Denlinger's children posed for this publicity photo back when their dad first opened the Red Caboose Motel, in 1970. In addition to the bunk beds, this remodeled car has a double bed, toilet, shower and sink, writing desk, and a television in the potbellied stove.

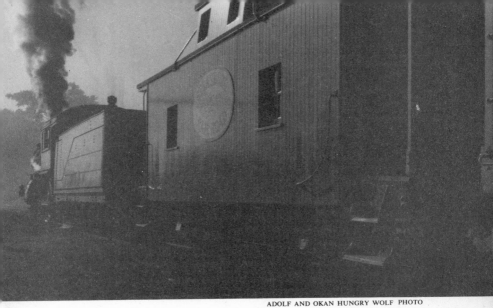

ADOLF AND OKAN HUNGRY WOLF PHOTO

Above, a bright autumn morning in Pennsylvania's Amish country sees this unbelievable yet real railroad scene: A coal-burning engine and a tiny, four-wheeled "bobber" caboose—painted bright red—have just delivered a modern freight car to a Conrail siding for later pickup by cabooseless freight. Oldest short line in America, the four-and-a-half mile Strasburg RR carries fare-paying passengers in the caboose, making this a genuine steam-powered mixed train, a living vestige of the past. *Below,* a unique set of windows brings cheerful light into this restored 1970 steel-bodied Conrail caboose, now operating on the short line New Hope & Ivyland by the name of "Closet Squirrel." Okan and editor Pat are having lunch at the spacious table, seated in luxurious, adjustable seats, mesmerized by the passing country scenery. One of this red caboose's bay windows is partly visible at the left.

AHW PHOTO

A northern Ontario snowstorm, seen from the cupola of Algoma Central Railway caboose 9517 in late winter of 1987. The Hearst station lights combine with snowflakes and clouds of steam from the adjacent passenger train's heating system to produce a photo flashback to an earlier time.   TIME EXPOSURE BY ADOLF AND OKAN HUNGRY WOLF

Above, ACR conductor Louie Mazzanello has lots of light and a comfortable space for his paper work aboard one of the road's six steel-bodied cabooses, or vans. Electric lights, stove and refrigerator are powered by a small gasoline generator attached beneath the caboose body. The gauge on the wall shows the amount of air pressure in the train's brake system. *Below,* ACR trainman Peter Domich has just coupled his freight train to our van and is now turning the angle cock to hook us into the train's air-brake system. In emergencies we could stop by tightening the chain on the manual brake wheel, up on our end platform, although this wheel is used mainly to keep the car in place once it has uncoupled from the train.

SELF-PORTRAIT BY ADOLF AND OKAN HUNGRY WOLF

Above, part of the efficient living space on ACR Van 9517 during the period that we lived aboard it. A propane cookstove is on the right, and an oil heater sits beyond it. Behind the camera are four bunks for sleeping; the car has enough chairs, benches and table space for such a crew to live, work and relax. The long metal pipe up at the ceiling is for hooking a portable telephone up to the ACR's trackside wires, a traditional form of railroad communication still used on this wilderness line. *Below,* upstairs, in the cupola of ACR 9517, having applesauce and chocolate cookies while watching the wild scenery from the depths of our overstuffed seats. The overhead cord controls the emergency brake, in case something doesn't look right on the train ahead.

OKAN HUNGRY WOLF PHOTO

Last of the Wild Cabooses—Algoma Central Railway No. 9517 sits on the "housetrack" at scenic Agawa Canyon, ready at any time to make the final encore for wooden cabooses on the adjacent main line.   SELF-PORTRAIT BY ADOLF AND OKAN HUNGRY WOLF

The Classic Caboose Scene: Conductor Roy H. Allen watches as his rear brakeman, George Vance, goes back with flag and fusees to protect the rear of their Southern Pacific freight train after making a stop in California's Tehachapi mountains, sometime around 1950. Modern radios and signals have eliminated the need for this important duty in train service.   PHOTO FROM ROCKY MOUNTAIN FREIGHT TRAIN MUSEUM

CHAPTER NINE

Railroad Lingo, Women Presidents, and Rhymes

Did you know a "bakehead" was a locomotive fireman, and a "throttle jerker" his engineer? If so, you are probably an old railroader, else a steady reader of *Railroad Magazine,* which sometimes printed lists of words and meanings unique to railroad life and was full of colorful railroad stories, like this one recounted by Freeman Hubbard:

> A beanery queen once inquired of her girl friend, "What became of that bakehead who was rushin' you last spring?" To which the girl friend responded: "Oh, Bill McGinnis? I give him the air. I overheard Bill tellin' his throttle jerker, 'She's lame on her left side an' she's got a flat wheel on her right, an' she 'ops around like an old goat jumpin' a ditch.' Well, I make a few sizzlin' remarks, an' then I learn too late that he's only talkin' about his engine."

A "beanery queen" was the waitress at a railroad crew's favorite restaurant (or beanery). Often she was single, as were —invariably—one or two members of the eating train crew. On every railroad there developed interesting plots revolving around these women, for the reasons described by Bozo Texino in the Missouri Pacific's employees' magazine:

> The company furnished employment to the boomers, and the beaneries furnished them with wives. The beanery kinds picked their hashers with all the skill of a Ziegfeld selecting the front row

of his chorus. Each gal was standard gauge, neither too wide nor too thin, with aurora borealis eyes. She had a body that Fisher couldn't duplicate in a thousand years and walked with more movements than the Baker valvegear on a big passenger jack. She had to be all this, so nobody would kick about the price of grub. The boomers fell harder for these gals than a pile-driver on a thirty-foot drop, and their love was neither platonic nor puppy. In those days a hasher wouldn't marry a tallowpot unless he could keep a white feather in the pop valve all the way over the division.

SOME COMMON RAILROAD TERMS

Air monkey   Air brake repairman.

Ashcat   Locomotive fireman; also called "bakehead," "tallowpot," "fireboy," etc.

Bad order   Car or locomotive needing repair; also called a "cripple."

Ballast scorcher   Speeding engineer.

Banjo   Fireman's shovel.

Battleship   Big locomotive, or any formidable female such as a landlady or mean wife.

Beans   A meal (as in "we stopped for beans").

Bedbug   Sleeping-car porter.

Big hole   As a verb: to instantly "dump" the air from a train's brake system, thus causing the fastest possible stop; as a noun: an emergency.

Big hook   Wrecking crane.

Bindle stiff   Hobo; also called a "boxcar tourist." "Bindle" refers to the common bundle of blankets carried on hoboes' backs.

Bird cage   Brakeman's signal lantern with protective wire.

Boomer   Railroad worker who drifts from one place to another, working on different lines and jobs.

Brass hat   Railroad official; long ago, some wore caps with brass nameplates and gold braid.

Bull   Railroad cop—the dreaded enemy of the bindle stiffs.

Car toad   Inspector or repairman of railroad cars, so called because of his squatting position while inspecting the underneaths of cars.

Catwalk   Wooden planks on top of freight cars on which brakemen had to walk.

Cow cage   Stockcar for cattle.

Croaker   Company doctor; also called "sawbones."

Crummy   Caboose; also called "buggy," "bouncer," "clown car," "shack," "parlor," and numerous other terms.

Deadhead   Any rail movement not earning income; a locomotive or car being hauled empty for use in another location; an employee being sent by the company to begin work somewhere else.

Dope   Compound used for cooling hotboxes; written orders for train and crew movements.

Doubleheader   A train with two engines and their crews.

Drag   A slow freight train; a heavy load.

Dude   Passenger conductor.

Eagle eye   Locomotive engineer; also called "hoghead" (engines are frequently "hogs"), "throttle jerker" and "runner" (among other things!).

Flag   An alias, often used by boomers to find work (if they had had trouble on a previous railroad, they would "work under a flag").

Gandy dancer   Track worker; the name derives from the varied bodily movements used while laying, adjusting and hammering tracks.

Goat   Switch engine.

Grease monkey   Car and locomotive oiler.

Greasy spoon   Low-grade beanery; its menu is a "switch list"; coffee is "java"; hotcakes are "gaskets"; beans are "torpedoes."

Groundhog   Brakeman; also called "herder," "shack."

Hand bomber   Steam locomotive whose coal had to be shoveled into the firebox manually (later engines had mechanical stokers).

Hash house   An acceptable beanery, generally better than a greasy spoon.

Highball   The signal for a train to get on out of town, given by raising the hand or lantern high above one's head and swinging it in an arc; comes from the era of signal posts with round metal balls, the highest point indicating a train had a free track ahead.

High iron   Main line.

Home guard   One who spent his life on a particular railroad; opposite of a boomer.

Hostler   Operator of locomotives around shops and roundhouses, usually a beginning fireman; also called "ashpit engineer."

Hotbox   Overheated journal on a car wheel.

Hotshot   A fast train; also called "manifest" and "merchandiser"; opposite of a drag.

Jack   Locomotive, especially a large one; also called "hog," "tea-kettle" and, most commonly, "engine"; called a "lokey" on logging railroads and a "unit" in the days of diesels.

Juice   Electric (as in "juice jack," and "juice line").

King   Yardmaster or, occasionally, conductor; "king snipe" is the foreman of a track gang.

Lightning slinger   Telegraph operator; also called "op."

Lizard scorcher   Chef on a dining car.

Make a joint   Couple cars together.

Markers   Signals on the rear of a train; flags or lamps displayed on the back of a caboose.

Merry-go-round   Engine turntable.

Mudhop   Yard clerk—the guy who has to take inventory of cars in the yards no matter what the weather.

Nut splitter   Shopman; machinist.

Oilcan   Tank car.

Old man   Superintendent, the highest official usually seen by rail workers.

Peddler   Local train making many stops; carrying cars with small shipments for numerous customers.

Pike   Railroad (as in "iron pike").

Pinhead   Yard switchman, from the days of link-and-pin couplers; also called "snake," "reptile," and "switch monkey."

Pud   Pickup and delivery; a railroad service.

Pull the air   To big hole from the conductor's end by pulling open the valve in a caboose.

Pusher   One or more engines on the back of a train, helping those up front.

Rawhider   One who is hard on men or equipment.

Ringmaster   Yardmaster, who is in charge of the whole switchyard "circus."

Rip track   Where cars and engines are repaired.

Rule G   One of twelve general railroad rules, this one forbids the use of liquor.

Sandhog   Workman on a tunnel or subway line.

Shoo-fly   Temporary track, usually built around an accident or washout.

Side-door pullman   Boxcar used by hoboes to steal a ride.

Skipper   Conductor; also called "brains," the "boss of shack."

Spot   To set a car at a specific place; also to take time out (as in "to go on spot").

Straphanger   Passenger without a seat, usually on commuter and subway trains.

Tin lizard   Early name for streamlined train.

Trick   Work shift (such as the "midnight trick").

Varnish   Passenger train; also a private railroad car.

Washout   Emergency stop signal; it is followed by a "big hole."

Whiskers   Seniority (as in "I didn't have enough whiskers").

Zulu   A family or emigrant outfit on a train, usually consisting of household furniture, tools, livestock and family members. At one time, this was a common way for people of the land to relocate.

Lest some of you old-timers take me to task about mistakes and omissions, let me point out that the above terms and definitions are only selections from the most common used over the past 150 years of railroading. Nearly every railroad had peculiar words and phrases of its own; sometimes even these varied among the crews. Workers from former times would be hard pressed to understand some of today's computer-oriented rail lingo, such as "highball the scanner," meaning a train has passed the trackside scanning device and no hot wheels have been found; "midtrain slaves," meaning helper engines, without crews, controlled electronically from the head end; or "dead-man's control," meaning a pedal on which a diesel engineer must keep pressure with his foot, or else it will warn him and then bring the train to a stop.

THE FEMALE PRESENCE

Of all the changes that have occurred on railroads, I think the one that would surprise old-time railroaders the most is the common presence today of women on train crews. In fact, occasional mainline trains operate with all-women crews—

engineer, conductor and brakeman (whoops, make that brake-person!).

Back in the steam days, women engineers and firemen were virtually unknown. As recently as 1960, the U.S. Census listed only eighty-five female engineers, most of them on private and industrial railroads. Union members wanted "no women!" They had rules forbidding them from joining, along with blacks and other minorities.

Two decades of social changes and legislation have brought women into most aspects of railway operation. On steam-powered tourist lines there are numerous women engineers and firers(!), showing everyone, belatedly, that it could have been done all along. In the Colorado Rockies, one husky young wife of a steam engine rebuilder dons coveralls and gets just as greasy as her mate, her skill and knowledge being considered equal by her fellow shop workers.

For a while, not long ago, the transcontinental Canadian National had a woman as president, and this was hailed far and wide as an example of new rights for women. Yet, several women presidents of smaller railroads were featured in a June 1935 issue of *Railroad Stories* (for many years another "flag" for *Railroad Magazine*).

An ex-trainman named Charles F. Carter took an interest in this subject and came up with an article called "Madame President." He said there were six of them at the time (over fifty years ago). He also named two women who were "chairmen" of boards of directors and six who were vice presidents. One railroad had fifty-two employees, of whom three were women vice presidents helping to run sixty-two miles of busy line.

It's not likely that any of these women were more dedicated to their jobs than Mrs. Lucy Rogers Walsh, president of the Rock Island Southern Railway. She and her husband built the railroad as a family venture right after they got married in 1908. The eighty-one miles of track connected Galesburg, Illinois, with the quad cities of Rock Island, Moline, and East Moline, Illinois, and Davenport, Iowa. When Mr. Walsh died suddenly, in 1932, his wife became boss of over thirty employees, who used 4 steam engines, 8 coaches and 111 freight cars to handle their railroad business. Serving under Mrs. Walsh as vice president and treasurer were two of her husband's brothers.

Susan Morning Star and Catherine Shirley were no doubt at the opposite end of the social scale from Mrs. Walsh when they became the first women to work on North American Railroads, hired in 1855 as "cleaners" on the Baltimore & Ohio. A 1930s United States census report listed 381,204 women employed by railroads—over a quarter million! Among them were 21 officials, 16 freight agents, 13 inspectors, 50 "foremen," 1,790 ticket and station agents, 16,122 telegraph operators, 289 "switchmen," and holders of several other positions. In Alabama, one woman was found to be hewing oak cross-ties for the Louisville & Nashville, producing from six to eight per day, using only an axe!

Manpower shortages caused by World War II forced many railroads to hire women. Most performed such mundane labor tasks as cleaning out passenger trains, wiping down locomotives or handling office work, but a few managed to get into more "dramatic" roles, including positions with regular train crews.

Around Philadelphia, for instance, the Reading line had a number of female "firemen" working on switchers over the vast industrial trackage. One switcher crew consisted of John and Lillian White; he was a twenty-year veteran working as engineer, she was his fireman. This combination was considered so unique that the couple was interviewed on national radio in January 1944, although there were some other husband-and-wife engine crews, as well.

Miss Verdie Pearl Harrison accepted a more "ladylike" job for that era when she graduated from high school in 1943 and became a night station agent and operator for the Louisville & Nashville at Cottondale, Florida. "I find it so interesting to sell tickets, check baggage, handle train orders and sling lightning [telegraph messages]," she told a reporter, "that I hope to be able to keep it up after the war."

She was said to have learned the work during a sixty-day

training period conducted by her uncle, L&N agent Charles C. Barlow, in order to train young girls to run railroad stations whose regular men were being sent off with the armed forces.

Loud complaints about female railroaders came from Jeff Davis, "King of the Hoboes," who said, "Next thing we know they'll be workin' on freight, an' what are yuh gonna do if a female shack [conductor] takes after yuh with a rollin' pin?"

THE RAIL WORKER

The railroader's life was a hard one and the men who worked on the trains were a varied lot, but most of them were imbued with a sense of the romance of the rails. J.A. Morris, a trackman who later became a Missouri Pacific roadmaster in Dermott, Arkansas, captured this life in the following poem printed years ago in a *Maintenance of Way Bulletin*:

A TRACKMAN'S LIFE

It's rain an' rain an' rain again, till all the
world's afloat,
An' workin' on this mud-line now, it
surely gets my goat.
A kingsnipe on the mid-line in the mud
an' slush an' rain,
The Old Man throwin' butterflies from
every bloomin' train.
There's sloppy joints in Johnson's cut;
the track is out of line.
"Go quick and cut the driftwood loose at
trestle Twenty-nine.
"The fence was down at Wilson's place,
when I passed there today,
"And all his cattle, sheep and hogs were
on the right-of-way."

The longest day must have an end, an'
men must have their rest,
An' comes the time, at evenin's close,
the time that I love best.
When car and tools are put away, an' I
get home once more,
An' see my Maggie's smilin' face beside
the kitchen door.
Then I wash up an' sit me down to
supper, pipin' hot,
An' cares take wing an' fly away, an'
troubles are forgot.
Then I smoke up while Maggie clears
away the supper things,
An' I start up the phonygraff, an' Harry
Lauder sings
"A Wee Hoose 'Mang the Heather: an'
the "Bonny Banks o' Doon,"
an' "Roamin' in the Gloamin'," now
that's a dandy tune.
My darlin's eyes grow misty—she's a
Scottish lass, you know—
An' me, my throat gets husky, an' I have
to cough, jus' so.

A trackman's life is hard, at best, his pay
is small beside,
But consciousness of work well done
should be a trackman's pride.
So give me my old pipe and I'll not envy
queens or kings,
With Maggie girl beside me here, while
Harry Lauder sings.

About 1930 E. S. Brooks, a boomer operator, trainmaster, etc. wrote a book called *Rail Rambles in Rhyme*, from which the following poem is taken.

A Mixed Run

Conductor's name Zwierzynski, flagman's
name O'Keefe,
Headman's name is Schnuckelheim, of whom
the con is chief;
The engineman's Nels Nelson, the fireman's
name La Voo;
That on the midnight local does constitute the
crew.

Zwierzynski hails from Poland, O'Keefe was
born in Cork,
Schnuckelheim from Neustadt came with
parents to New York;
Nels Nelson came from Sweden, "Land of
the Midnight Sun";
His fireman came from sunny France to fire a
midnight run.

The little red caboose behind the train; to
them was home
With coffee pot and frying pans, blankets,
brush and comb
That hung beside a looking-glass suspended
by a chain
And swung in perfect rhythm with the motion
of the train.

Here is a poem by Douglas Ward that captures the world of
the solitary rail worker:

Second Trick in the Desert

Down yonder in the sand cliffs
    I hear the Navajo drums
Beatin' out their evenin' songs
    As twilight softly comes.
The stars shine so clear and bright

And hang so low, it seems
I could reach up and pick a few
   To wrap around my dreams.

The Morse wires hum a lonely
tune,
   The dispatcher's phone is still;
The tingle of the soft laughter floats
   From the shacks below the hill.
Sittin' here in peaceful reverie,
   With God's world all vast and
still,
I know it's just one step to heaven
   From this Arizona hill.

CHAPTER TEN

Notes from Some Father and Son Train Trips

Little Railway Stations
Along a vibrant track
See trains forever going
And always coming back.

The rails are live and eager,
They stretch and curve the bend
Through pulsing, purple distance
On quests that have no end.

But lonely little stations
That wait beside the track
See only people going
And people coming back.

—ZOE BROCKMAN

So, what do you suppose a fellow like me does to take a break, after sitting aboard an old caboose and writing all winter? Does the poem that opens this chapter give you any idea? Can you imagine how it is for me to look out of these car windows and to suddenly yearn to hear those steel wheels underneath me roll?

In the Canadian Rockies, we're pretty fortunate, because we can go for a dramatic passenger train ride any day we wish to. The Canadian Pacific main line goes right through world-famous Banff National Park on its way across the Rockies; once a day, a classic passenger train follows that line in each direction. Sometimes we just ride that train for a few hours, to get the urge out of our systems. But, as its name, *The Canadian,* implies, it runs clear across the country, not just through the Rockies. And when I ride to some faraway place, such as Vancouver, Toronto or Montreal, my urge feels much more satisfied.

In fact, Okan and I have lately taken to making at least one annual trans-Canada trip by train, going first-class, sleeping in an upper and lower berth, eating our meals in the diners. Getting photos and stories for our series of railway books and calendars more than justifies the expenses of our travels. For Okan, the trips have become "mainline schoolwork." For a kid used to learning from correspondence courses, these train journeys are like seminars. Among the topics covered are history, economy, social studies, transportation, geography and—of course—sociology and psychology, for it affords many opportunities for close-up studies of interesting people! Please consider our example and take a kid that you know for a train journey!

Did I leave you wondering why *The Canadian* is such a special train, aside from the spectacular scenery that it travels through? It is because its equipment is vintage 1954, built when the train itself was first introduced. Although the cars have been rebuilt and modernized since then, a trip aboard the streamlined and aluminum-sided train is like a journey back in time. There's a much different atmosphere than aboard modern LRCs (Light, Rapid, Comfortable) and Amcoaches. For us, it's the luxurious equivalent of traveling aboard cabooses. It helps us to know that there's not another such streamlined domeliner still operating in daily service anywhere else in the world.

Of course, for a couple of caboose owners like us, there is no substitute for the real thing. We'd choose an old, grimy "crummy" over the glass-topped dome cars of *The Canadian*, anytime. Because of our work, we sometimes have our wish fulfilled. We've been on cabooses from coast to coast, from logging trains on the Pacific Coast to a narrow-gauge plow-extra on the island of Newfoundland. A few times we've even lived aboard them. Here are some highlights from those trips.

For Okan's seventh birthday (he was born in '73), we got to ride through the rain forest that runs along coastal Washington over the private line of Rayonier Incorporated. Originally built by the two Polson Brothers in 1903, this remote operation first lured me as a teenager with its half-dozen big steam engines that were then still in operation. For cabooses, the line had flat cars with metal railings, with a little "shack" at one end.

For Okan's "birthday ride" there was a big, old Baldwin diesel (steam's been long gone), plus a railed-in flatcar, although its shack—with a cupola and a fresh coat of yellow paint—was much nicer than the old ones. Passing neither towns nor people for most of the day, the crew let us feel "right at home" on the train, handling the throttle, blowing the horn (an unusually musical one) and sitting upstairs in the caboose. Those are now historical memories for Okan and me, since the rail line was completely abandoned a few seasons later.

We rode another private working railroad out on the Canadian prairies. Again we traveled through isolated country, reaching the end of the line at a lakehead where there are no roads. Known as the GWWD (Greater Winnipeg Water District), this line has a pretty bright future, being owned by the city of Winnipeg and required to service its water system. The train we rode on was very vintage and unique.

For one thing, it had only a two-man crew, both veterans of more than thirty years, on the line. Gerald Sedo ran the engine, which preceded his arrival on the GWWD by quite some time. No. 100 was bought new in 1946, making it some kind of record holder for length of service on the same railroad, especially among diesels. It is just a little forty-four-tonner, not much bigger than the six-wheeled steamers it helped replace.

On this trip, Okan and I preferred the caboose especially because it was a relative to ours, bought secondhand from CP Rail about the same time that we got ours. Painted plain yellow and stripped down inside to make it functional, this car recently replaced another caboose built in the 1890s!

Jimmy Landry, our cigar-smoking trainman, let us sit up in the cupola most of the way, preferring to stay downstairs at his desk, doing the "paperwork," which included reading an Irving Wallace novel called *Miracle*.

Between the engine and our caboose was a train of three cars that made this run most unique. There was a "ramp car," home-made and strange, rolling on a set of antique arch-bar trucks, of the kind outlawed on main lines in the 1930s. It carried a modern, yellow tractor-machine for the track crew along the line. Jimmy said the weird car was actually constructed from the tender frame of one of the original steam engines.

Our train looked like a real classic after we dropped that car off. There remained two aged flatcars and a yellow, wooden boxcar of 1890s style, plus our caboose and the yellow-painted engine, its silver roof reflecting the sunlight. Any transportation museum would be proud to have that collection.

Whenever Okan and I get to travel clear across the country aboard *The Canadian,* we have a favorite destination out in the farmlands not too far from Toronto. Another distant relative of our cabooses waits for us there—former CP Rail No. 437187. It belongs to our friend Jim Brown. A lifelong train rider and photographer, Jim wishes his job would give him more time to spend aboard the old car. It's a pretty cozy one, with electric lights and heating, refrigerator and TV, even a telephone. What job does this train enthusiast have, you may wonder? He is di-rector of railway operations for Toronto's very busy GO Transit, which has numerous modern trains in frequent commuter service.

THE NORTH CONWAY LIVING RAIL MUSEUM

In the picturesque White Mountain country of New Hamp-shire, we visited some caboose owners whose cars are still parked in an active railroad yard. Not only that, there's also a century-old station and roundhouse nearby, plus two lively steam engines.

The caboose owners pay rent to the Conway Scenic Railroad for their trackage space; the line's president, Dwight A. Smith, parks his private passenger car there, in the same way. Altogether, there are twelve privately owned rail vehicles in the North Conway yard, including seven cabooses, three snow flangers, a reefer and the coach. This is model railroading on the ultimate scale!

Blanche and Howard Audibert own former Central Vermont caboose No. 4011, a red, wooden classic built in 1910. "It's a 'his and hers,' " said Blanche enthusiastically when I asked about it. "I love the car; I only wish we could spend more time on it." The couple has a bit of traveling to do each time they pay it a visit, since their primary home is in St. Petersburg, Florida, where Howard is an award-winning architect.

"It was a long-held dream for me to own a caboose," said Howard, after inviting Okan and me aboard for a visit. "I've chased trains all my life and photographed them. I can't think of a better vacation home."

Howard's skills were put to the test when he redesigned the caboose's interior to make a pleasant home for two. He had to plan carefully in order to fit all the conveniences they wanted into a space of about eight feet by thirty.

There's now a small sitting room where the conductor used to work, a dining space where the stove used to be and an efficient kitchen beneath the cupola. One closet holds a toilet, the other a shower ("you have to kind of back your way into them"). Upstairs, the cupola seats now fold down into two narrow ("but cozy") sleeping berths. The little home has wall-to-wall carpeting, stereo music and ample electric lights, even in the closets! Pretty luxurious to us, living with kerosene lights and wood heat.

"We heard about a fellow up here who had five old cabooses for sale," said Howard, when I asked how he got the car. "He was starting up a roadside cheese-selling business with them, but when that didn't take off quite like he'd expected, he gave up and sold out. He was asking $3,500 apiece for the cars, but we got that down to $2,500 and had the pick of the lot, besides. Of course, this was back in the mid-seventies; caboose prices have gone up since then, and you don't see as many for sale."

The couple became so pleased with their unique vacation

home that they persuaded Howard's brother and his wife to move in "next door." They now own a reefer (Bangor & Aroostook refrigerator car No. 7574), which makes an even more unique retreat than a caboose—especially since architect brother Howard designed an interior that maintains the outside of the car's historical integrity, which is a requisite factor for the living-museum rail yard of the Conway Scenic.

To avoid cutting holes for windows into the solid walls of the reefer, Howard's plans called for skylights to replace four square doors on the car's roof, originally used for stocking the car with ice. In addition, sliding glass doors were installed on the inside, accessible from the outside by opening the original, insulated doors. On the "far side," a wooden porch leads up to this door, with potted plants adding a touch of life and color.

The "near side" of these private cars faces the old freight yard; owners are required to keep their cars looking authentic. But since they are parked on the "last track," with only a tree-lined meadow and golf course beyond, the owners have expanded there with additions such as wooden patios, barbecue pits, tent trailers and big umbrellas. Looking down that side during our visit, we had images of a caboose-KOA.

Neighbors at the other end of the Audiberts' are John and Betty-Jean Egan, who live year-round only thirty miles away. John must be about the only man who works all week long on cabooses as a conductor, only to spend his weekends and vacations aboard another one. What's more, he made his first working trip as a brakeman, back in 1949, on this very car. You can't get much more intimate with your vacation home than that!

The Egans' car is a classic, built for the Grand Trunk Western in 1915. Its frame is supported by truss rods (the things hoboes are supposed to have made their beds on), a rare reminder of early-day railroad technology.

This is actually John Egan's third caboose; someone else still owned it when he bought his first one. That first one was damaged in a fire set by vandals (a constant threat to caboose owners, especially those who don't live aboard or next door). He traded the remains of that car to Dwight Smith for a nice little one from the Chesapeake & Ohio Railroad. When he got the chance to buy the one on which he made his first trip, he sold the C&O car to one of the Conway Scenic Railroad's locomotive engineers.

To bring this story full circle, John got to work as conductor and trainmaster aboard his first caboose during the time that Okan and I were there. Once a year, the Conway Scenic Railroad has a "Railfan Day," during which they bring out and run much of their antique equipment.

Egan's first caboose had been made available to a local model railroad group, for meetings and layout space, in return for its restoration. It showed up on "Railfan Day" in a new coat of red paint, although its interior was still in the process of being refurbished. Because of its condition, the car made only one brief trip, and that behind a diesel, but John rode it and gave the signals while it was being switched by a pair of steam engines in the yard. Since he actually worked on this car back in the steam era, imagine the feelings of déjà vu he must have had that recent day!

THE NEW HOPE STEAM RAILROAD

While working on this book, Okan and I thought it would be ideal if we could deliver the finished manuscript to our publisher aboard a caboose. Unfortunately, Conrail freight trains running in and out of New York City were among the earlier trains to lose their cabooses, so such a trip could not be made easily. However, our editor, Pat Golbitz, has a country home in historic New Hope, Pennsylvania, where the shortline New Hope & Ivyland does have cabooses. When Pat invited Okan and me to spend the weekend, I wrote to this railroad and explained the situation.

By return mail, members of the New Hope Steam Railroad and Museum advised me that they could make a caboose, hooked to the back of their regular excursion train, available to the three of us for a "private outing." Not only that, but the car would be one formerly operating on Conrail, a "recently restored model of 1970."

I had to read that date several times to believe it. A restored *1970* caboose? My God, could I be that old, already? Okan was born just three years later, yet the car was already sounding like some kind of relic.

It turned out that the caboose serves as a "private car" for the McHugh brothers, who own the railroad. This family rescued the branch line a few years ago, after it fell on hard times and was threatened with abandonment. In addition to providing limited freight service and using some tracks to store their railroad-contracting equipment, the McHughs allow weekend use of their line by the nonprofit museum group, which has several old cars and three steam engines. This group also maintains New Hope's preserved 1890s station and adjacent freight house, both located across the alley from the old Delaware Canal, where connecting trips can be made aboard mule-drawn barges.

The 1970 caboose was indeed restored, even customized. Its freshly painted steel interior included wall-to-wall carpeting, high-backed swivel chairs (firmly mounted to the floor) and a set of tall, oblong windows which made for good viewing of the scenic route. In place of an upstairs cupola, this modern car has a pair of floor-level bay windows, from which we watched the train curving ahead.

Museum volunteer Bill Coffey showed us aboard, although we were left alone once the train started. A tall, genial man, Bill retired just a few years ago from Conrail. "I just can't seem to stay away from the railroad," he said with a smile, explaining his busy involvement. He works as engineer, conductor, restorer and maintenance man.

THE CABOOSE KING

Don Denlinger is a much different kind of railroad jack-of-all-trades; Okan and I call him the "Caboose King." The forty cabooses that make up his Red Caboose Motel, in Strasburg, Pennsylvania, got him listed in the *Guinness Book of World Records* as owner of the largest private collection of real cabooses.

When Okan and I rode down from New York aboard Amtrak's famous *Broadway Limited* to visit him, he came to meet us at the nearby station in Lancaster, wearing a white shirt, vest and station agent's cap.

It didn't take Don and me long to laugh about the two opposite extremes that we experience in our daily lives with cabooses. The four belonging to our family are privately maintained, have varying, personal interior arrangements, and are seldom seen by anyone other than our family and friends. By contrast, Don's forty cars are seen daily by hundreds, often thousands, some of whom leave disappointed when they learn that reservations for a stay must be made far ahead.

"Everyone from kids to grandparents gets a thrill out of sleeping aboard a real caboose," he said, demonstrating no loss in enthusiasm after all that the cars have put him through. "I could handle a lot more people, but local zoning laws won't let me add anymore cabooses!"

Owning such a fleet of cabooses was not exactly his goal in life, Don Denlinger told us during the drive from the station. "A friend dared me to bid on a few that the Penn Central had up for offers," he explained. So he sent in a figure so low that he thought they might let him have one or two, at best. Those, he had thought to incorporate into his heritage-oriented Mill-Bridge Craft Village, which he was then developing in the midst of the Pennsylvania Dutch country.

A midwinter phone call suddenly brought chaos to Denlinger with news that his bid had been accepted for all *nineteen* cabooses on offer. He was expected to pay for them right away and to move them immediately thereafter. Not a small task, considering the value and weight of all that steel. From that day on, those cabooses have been at the center of his life. These were some of his trials and tribulations:

- A railroad official said he could park the cars on an empty siding just a mile from where they were. The railroad sent a switch engine to move them the one mile, but he was charged for the minimum distance—seventy-five miles— times nineteen!
- A different official said there was a law requiring formal leases for private cars to be left on railroad property; not having one, he was given twenty-four hours to move off. While he tried to arrange for some financing, the railroad sent another switcher to move the cars back to the yard; he got another bill for moving each of the nineteen cars seventy-five more miles.
- After convincing skeptical bank officials to back his idea of turning the cabooses into a motel, he located a shop with its own railroad siding that was willing to make some basic repairs on the cars, including sandblasting and rust proofing, to start them on their way to becoming motel units; unfortunately, the siding was served by a different railroad; to get his cabooses there, he had to pay *both* rail companies for the minimum seventy-five miles—times nineteen, of course.
- With the bank money, he bought a farm suitable for his purpose and conveniently located alongside the main line of the widely known, steam-powered Strasburg Railroad. But when he went to purchase used track materials, he found those available for sale to be frozen solidly to the ground of an old railroad yard.
- It took great effort and determination for himself and two others to pry loose the required 500 ties and thirty tons of steel rails, along with track fittings. Then, as they were ready to leave with this load, a railroad official came, saying that half the ties were too good to be sold and must be given back.
- To help solve the need for sewer and water, he bought three used railroad tank cars. Preparing them to meet standards for such underground service, hired workmen were spraying

the insides with a special compound when a spark from a dropped light bulb created a fatal explosion that blew one workman outside and clear through an overhead metal roof.

• The time finally came when cabooses and motel land were ready to be combined. The move required coordinated efforts and timing by several teams of men and heavy equipment. Denlinger had to work with three different railroads, the section men of one having to tear apart its main line in order to get the cabooses onto their final site.

• The first hitch in the final move came when the train crew of railroad No. 2 refused to wait for those of railroad No. 1 until he offered to pay them overtime, from his own pocket, for the extra hours. Otherwise all the complicated arrangements would have been delayed one whole day.

• A brief highlight of the caboose move occurred when railroad No. 3 took over. No. 3 was the local Strasburg Rail Road, which sent one of its steam engines. Denlinger got photos for posterity showing his string of nineteen cabooses under smoke and steam.

• But the thrill of steam faded soon after, when his strange train derailed on the sharp curve that had been built up to the motel site. Unable to move the cars forward or backward, the steamer was left stranded on the wrong side—it needed to go beyond the curve in order to reach water. Without it, the boiler was in danger of blowing up. Shutting the engine down on the main line would have been illegal. A nearby fire department finally came to the rescue with a water truck.

• Eventually the cars did reach their final resting places, though Denlinger's problems were far from over. For instance, he'd bought a load of fiberglass shower stalls, but now found that they wouldn't fit through the narrow *steel* doorways. He ended up having welders cut holes into each car's side, put the showers through and then weld the holes shut again. You can't hide seams like that on a steel body.

"Still, those first nineteen cabooses were the easy ones," Denlinger told us with a look of pained experience. "At least I was able to have all of them brought in at once, and over railroad tracks. The other twenty-one came here by truck, traveling on highways, and that's where you *really* start to run into problems!"

These later cabooses came from several railroads and private owners. For instance, one day an elderly lady phoned and said her husband had just died. They had been operating a catering service from a caboose parked at a still active railroad station. Suddenly Amtrak wanted the caboose moved, immediately. Denlinger could have it free, just for the taking.

He phoned a trailer-moving outfit, whose boss said, "No problem! We're used to fifty- and sixty-foot units; yours is only thirty." Denlinger shook his head as he recalled, "Those long trailers he was used to hauling were like paper milk cartons compared to that caboose with its twenty-five tons of solid steel!"

When the trucker got the caboose settled on his three-axle trailer, its springs were just about upside-down. "He swore and threatened to sue me if anything went wrong because of it."

The planned route was changed so as to avoid taking the precarious load through large towns and cities. Denlinger followed behind, expecting to see the load snap at any time, with his caboose tumbling into traffic.

"Then we reached the interstate bridge. The supervisor came out, took one look at that sagging load and demanded to see our papers. 'Papers? What papers?' I asked him. Turns out that it was *my* responsibility—as the hiring operator—to obtain proper permits, which I hadn't done."

Denlinger was told that it might take several days to get the proper documents, during which time his caboose would stay "right where it was." Underneath it sat a truck and trailer for which he was paying by the hour. A quick check had proven the load to be overweight, overheight, *and* too low. These things were not permitted even with documents.

"I got frantic, so I tried to tell this official how the caboose was to become part of a heritage project for future generations of caboose lovers and fans. Suddenly, he said to me, 'Are *you* the fellow from that Red Caboose Motel over in Strasburg?' When I told him I was, he went on, 'I brought my grandson there to stay, for a special treat, and he hasn't stopped talking about it yet!' Then he called out a police escort to lead us and the caboose over the bridge, telling me that he hoped we'd have no further trouble, which we didn't.''

Along with all the standard-sized cabooses, Denlinger also has a couple of small ones—''bobbers''—that ride on only four wheels. You would think that these would have been the easiest of his fleet to move, yet they caused him the most trouble. For one thing, their wheels didn't come off, like those on the bigger cars, so that they sat up quite high on the moving trucks.

As Denlinger was having the first of these two midgets driven home, their outfit reached a busy highway overhead that was too low; there was no way to turn around and go back. The truck driver made a drastic suggestion, telling him to go borrow a saw in order to cut off the cupola. Seeing no other choice, he did so, but with a heavy heart. It was like breaking up the best part of a piece of furniture in order to bring it into the house.

After removing the windows, Denlinger got inside to saw the corner posts, following the directions of the driver, who said he would then lower the cupola down inside. Unfortunately, the driver didn't realize how sturdy the little car was until the posts were all cut and the heavy cupola tore from his grip, nearly crushing Denlinger, below.

The second ''bobber'' was hauled over a different route so that its cupola didn't have to be cut down. Instead, this one developed bottom troubles, right on a crowded main street.

''We were going through this small town,'' Denlinger recalls, ''me following right behind, when the caboose suddenly lurched sideways. Its rotting floorboards had given out from all the bouncing on the roads. The body crashed down over its own frame and wheels; I expected to see it fall over into a row of shiny cars parked along the curb, or even into a store!

"Even worse, my fourteen-year-old son was riding up on top of the caboose! He was guiding electric wires over its roof with a wooden pole." Fortunately, the boy was quick enough to grab hold of the roof and hang on until the body settled firmly on its wheels, still standing upright. After tying it down with chains, they continued the trip without further mishap.

Staying in a motel-caboose feels totally different from riding aboard one that is still in service, or even from sitting in our own, at home. Because of curtains on the windows, and the small room at each end, Okan and I missed the airiness and open views. But we were intrigued by the night-light up in the inaccessible cupola, where some of the plumbing fixtures are also hidden. There was a small shower and toilet underneath the cupola. The most unusual aspect of the room was its TV, mounted inside an old pot-bellied heater. We saw more channels here than at any other place we'd been, an impressive fact for us, since we live at home without television.

For those of you thinking of getting a caboose of your own, Don Denlinger offers the following advice:

1. "Keep in mind that *buying* the caboose is the easiest part. The hard part is moving it and setting it up.
2. When you start to restore it, do it right! Shortcuts will make you sorry later. In the case of steel cabooses, that means sanding right down to bare metal, everywhere, and removing *all* the rust. Next, apply a good coat of rust-proofing. When you just paint over the bad spots, they only get worse.
3. Don't try to save money by doing it improperly yourself; hire a professional."

He said there is not much difference in general upkeep between wooden cabooses and those made of steel (most of his are the latter). "Main thing about the steel ones is that every time you need to do body work, it means hiring a welder. You can't just nail a piece of plywood over a bad spot for a patch."

One important discovery was that adding wooden interiors to steel-bodied cars helped a lot in maintaining moisture control. A big problem is that the steel roofs really heat up in summer and take a long time to cool down. Denlinger installed air conditioning in all his cars, right from the start.

He also experimented with a couple of caboose roofs by having styrofoam sprayed over them. On the steel car, this cut the air conditioning bills in half. On the wooden one, it cut down the need for heating. Over the styrofoam he put a black, rubberized roofing material that not only looks authentic but is guaranteed to stop leaks (a major problem with our own old roofs). This stuff is considered state-of-the-art railroad car roofing, but is so expensive that Denlinger has not found funds to do the other thirty-eight.

When we asked if he considered any of the cabooses "his own," he answered, "No, I'm too busy keeping everyone entertained with the whole fleet." But his personal favorite is the so-called "Honeymoon Caboose," which has red velvet paper on its walls and ceiling, a special love seat, plus a queen-sized bed with ornate brass railings.

SOME GREAT CABOOSE RIDES

The highlight of our visit to Strasburg was a short ride that Okan and I took on its railroad, our first in a four-wheeled "bobber." This short line (oldest in the country) still handles an occasional car of freight, although its main business is tourist traffic. Once a week you can ride in the caboose of a genuine, steam-powered mixed train for a nine-mile round trip.

If you're looking for a more dramatic caboose trip, consider riding the state-owned Cass Scenic Railroad down in West Virginia. Its powerful geared locomotives run up to the top of Bald Mountain using switchbacks and eleven percent grades. If you want to get really serious, about $650 will get you a private round-trip—including engine and caboose—and home-cooked meals can be arranged!

An equally exciting, but longer and far more historic train trip can be had on the Cumbres & Toltec Scenic Railroad, which is jointly owned by the states of New Mexico and Colorado. This narrow-gauge route was originally built by the Denver & Rio Grande during the glamorous silver mining days of the late 1800s, but is preserved now as an operating museum, still using original equipment. With family or friends, you could charter your own train—including caboose and steam engine—to haul you right over the summit of the Rockies, crossing Cumbres Pass at 10,015 feet!

In the Maritimes of Canada you can sleep aboard a caboose while it is parked in a rail yard, then the next day you can ride it behind a train pulled by steam. The Salem & Hillsborough Railroad, running on a branch line south of Moncton, New Brunswick, is so removed from tourist places that it offers several cars for low-priced accommodations.

Up in the Pacific Northwest there's another chance for a private caboose ride. The Mount Rainier Scenic Railroad runs out of Elbe, Washington, over a still active logging line, providing steam- and diesel-powered trips along the base of its namesake.

You can rent their caboose for a kid's birthday party—including catered meals—at a low cost if you leave it parked in the yard, or for slightly more if you want it coupled to the back of a train. If you really want to make your ride spectacular, hire two engines to pull the caboose, then sit in the cupola and watch the lively action! Finally, you could add the luxurious observation car, also for hire, then hold a simultaneous, steam-powered, his-and-hers party! Afterward, enjoy a unique supper at a local restaurant made from a converted caboose and passenger cars, then stay at a cozy bed-and-breakfast that includes cabooses for accommodations.

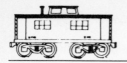

CHAPTER ELEVEN

Last of the Wild Cabooses

Its wooden sides are painted reddish-orange—kind of faded now, for many years have passed since the last coat was added. On each flank there is a large white logo showing the encircled silhouette of a Bear. This is van No. 9517; we're on the Algoma Central Railway, whose well-deserved slogan reads, "Route of the Black Bear."

The ACR serves about three hundred miles of northern Ontario wilderness, providing vital services to places where there are no roads. Camping gear, building supplies, guns and canoes are among items commonly seen in the baggage cars of this railroad's passenger trains. And yes, folks, it's a line that, in the late 1980s, still operates its *own* passenger services—without VIA or Amtrak!

At the time of this writing, the ACR also stands out for having the last couple of wooden cabooses known to be in mainline service around North America. One of them—No. 9517—has become a friend and occasional home for Okan and me during our train trips across Canada. We obtained permission to make a photo documentary of life around this old van (the accepted term for a caboose on the ACR), so now, this last chapter is being written while staying and traveling aboard what we call the "last of the wild cabooses."

It's the beginning of March 1987 as we sit aboard the 9517, which is parked on "the old coach track" in the yard at Hawk Junction. This place has as much character as its name implies

—a remote town with mostly railroad men and their families. It is one of the few places along the ACR that can be reached by highway (a two-laner with long, lonely stretches, prone to heavy fogs from the nearby Great Lakes, and sometimes impassable because of dreadful winter blizzards).

Hawk Junction is the ACR's only division point. Trains from here run in three different directions: south, to Sault Sainte Marie (called the "Soo"), the railway's headquarters and home of a vital steel industry; north, to the French-Canadian lumber town of Hearst; and, westward, over a winding branch, to Wawa and Michipicoten Harbour on the north shore of Lake Superior, sources of the ACR's mainstay ore traffic for the steel industries at the Soo.

Without these trains and their crews, Hawk Junction would be just another pretty place in the "bush," one of countless sites on the shores of "bush lakes." Virtually every family living around Hawk Junction has someone working for the railroad, and it's been that way for so long that half of the railroad workers, or more, are related to one another. Several fellows are fourth generation Hawk Junction railroad men, which fact tends to be a major source of inspiration for them.

It took our freight train all day to get up here from Sault Sainte Marie, although company timetables list the distance as being only 164.6 miles. There were no other towns in between and, after a few miles, no more highways or connecting roads —just lakes, forests and scatterings of cabins, often sitting alone, though sometimes grouped into vacation villages or small logging and mining camps. At this time of year, most places are still boarded up for the winter, the human population along the ACR being not only small but also highly fluctuating, depending on the season.

The center of Hawk Junction is an open square, with the station and ACR yard to one side and a handful of buildings on the other. Most important of these is the pub, on the lower floor of what used to be the town's two-story clapboard hotel. Here, friends and fellow railroaders meet in the evenings over beers, often to discuss the day's catch made by those who had a few extra hours for fishing, else the game count, when the hunting season is open. The count involves mainly moose and edible birds, with an occasional bear, deer being absent from the area. In the winter, pub discussions often concern furs caught by local trappers, of which there are a number even among the railroad men.

A propane-powered wall lamp is lighting up the table where Okan and I are writing our notes. We have just finished a meal of rice and vegetables, cooked by Okan on the van's propane stove. It sits on a shelf against the wall, right next to the oil heater and across the aisle from the chairs where we sit. Lots of places to sit, in fact; besides the four cozy cupola seats, our bunks and a small bench, we have four "conductor's chairs," of the kind that seafarers would credit to the captain. On some railroads, that latter title happened to be a nickname for the train conductor.

It was last fall that we first saw the 9517, parked on this same track, as we came through Hawk Junction on the passenger train during a photographing trip. This is Hawk Junction's "spare van," called for occasional work trains or when one of the ACR's six modern steel vans needs a substitute. Down at the Soo, No. 9502 serves the same purpose.

These are the last seasons of work for the two veterans; steel-bodied replacements are expected at any time. Right now, there is no shortage of good used ones on the market, for sale by their owners for a fraction of what they cost to build.

The idea of making a photo documentary of this caboose was well received by Newell Mills, superintendent of the Algoma Central Railway, whose permission got us aboard here. Train photographers have usually focused their interests on locomotives and head-end shots, leaving caboose life less-than-well-docu-mented. Mills shares our fondness for cabooses, having gained experience for his present job during some twenty years as an ACR brakeman and conductor, back when vans like this were the crews' second homes.

A mop leaning against the back platform tells you this caboose is regularly kept up, in spite of its fading paint, scuffed sides and tears in the worn roofing. Trainmaster Greg Lowe brought us in, helped light the heater and fill up the two water jugs, then handed us the key and said, "you can lock up if you want to go into town." He also hooked up mantles to two of the propane lamps and showed us how to keep them lit—modern technology for Okan and me, living at home with kerosene.

Distracted from writing for a bit by the sound of nearby revving diesel motors, we went up into the cupola to watch the evening's final train activity in the yard. First, a set of four units moved from the shops up to the fuel and sand facilities, where the hostlers prepared them for tonight's south-bound freight. Then, a short freight came in from the north behind two more units, which did a bit of switching before parking at the shop. They'll be joining the other four on tonight's train, whose northward counterpart will bring up a similar set of six units by early to-morrow morning.

We're used to enjoying nice scenery from our cupola windows at home, but never live railroad action like this. From the cupola, we also watched Carman Kenny Bain, the light from his lantern showing his progress in checking out the wheels and brakes of the night freight. Now and then the light disappeared, as he crawled between the cars for a better look. No wonder he says the job is much tougher in winter, when snows are often waist deep.

Kenny was here to visit with us a little while ago, before we went up in the cupola. A cheerful young fellow, blondish curls coming out from beneath his orange hard hat; born and raised in Hawk Junction. A real fisherman, from the sounds of it, he goes out to the waters nearly every day (a man true to Okan's liking!). He says he starts before daylight, first checking his minnow traps, from which he gets his own bait plus a few extra bucks from the sale of the surplus. After that, he goes out in his boat to fish until early afternoon (mostly in Hawk Lake, a short walk from here). At three, he goes to work in the railroad yard.

* * *

We were just now getting ready to head for bed when there was a knock on the side of the van. It was Kenny, stopping by to say goodnight. He brought us a real timely gift: a one-and-a-half-pound lake trout, cleaned, frozen and perfect for tomorrow night's meal.

"I know what it's like to be out on the road in a van," he said in a neighborly fashion. "My dad's been a conductor on the ACR since before I was born." He named several other family members working on the railway, including a brother who's an operator and another who maintains the locomotives at the shop. Along with the fish, Kenny left jars of home-canned relish and beets, a tiny container of cooking oil, plus salt and pepper wrapped in bits of tinfoil. There's a closet between this table and our bunks, inside which is the van's full set of cookware and eating utensils. Looks like we're in for a caboose feast, sometime to-morrow. Right now, we're both beat from a *long* day of trains (seventeen hours), so we'll head for bed.

A few minutes past noon the next day: We're back in the cupola, looking out through all the windows, just like we do at home. But this time, we're hooked to the back of a freight train, waiting to roll. What an exciting feeling, after a long winter at home of looking from cabooses that never go anywhere.

We slept well last night, warm and cozy in our lower bunks, having bought a pair of sleeping bags on sale at Sears, back at the Soo (in a place called Station Mall, owned by the ACR and located at the very end of its trackage). Luckily, the bunks already had pillows, since I don't sleep well without one. That they look rather "well used" doesn't matter, since we always carry our own pillow cases when traveling.

It was quiet in the yard last night, nothing rolled on the dozen or so tracks after the southbound freight left near midnight. Even the station was locked up afterward, with just a couple of lights left on. We were the only ones at the outskirts of town, with many miles of wilderness beyond us.

I haven't mentioned that it's been snowing all morning! Early March snowstorms are often the worst ones for railroad operations, since the snow usually comes down in big wet flakes that freeze solid during the night. If there's any accumulation, the result can be solid chunks that defy snowplow blades and can even make wheels climb up over the rails.

Just met the conductor, Louis Mozzonello, who says we'll be going as soon as the branch train for Michipicoten Harbour leaves and gives us a clear track. He's upset about the delay, because we'll have the passenger train coming up behind us before too long. The train's an hour from Hawk Junction right now, and the crew won't want to be delayed by our freight.

We photographed two trains this morning before we even had a chance for breakfast. First was the night freight, up from the Soo with its six big engines. The ground trembled when it came into the yard; several windows and metal things vibrated inside here, especially when the train pulled up even with us, over on the main line.

Soon after the night train got in, our crew from yesterday headed back down to the Soo. They'll have another long trip, doing all the switching at sidings along the way so that the night freight can roll right on through. A lot of the freight from these sidings is pulpwood, used to make paper, though out west we'd call the same stuff "fenceposts" and use it accordingly.

Between trains, we visited inside the station, where it's warm and friendly. Two operators sat by a big bay window, right in front of the main line, fielding telephone calls, radio reports from train crews and train orders from dispatchers down in the Soo. All the while, they carried on a lively banter with each other and everyone else inside the station, including other staff, the night-train crew "booking in" and the visitors from "away out in the Rockies." Here's truly the heart of Hawk Junction, where everything that's going on is sure to be known.

Suddenly a buzzer sounded loudly in the midst of all this activity, meaning there was a passenger wanting service back at the waiting-room window. A two-story, red-brick station, with

busy operators and an active waiting room is only one of several
vintage scenes found along the ACR, but not much of anywhere else.

That particular passenger, by the way, was a fellow going
forty miles down the line to his fishing cabin. Outside the station
stood his pickup truck, filled with material and supplies he was
bringing along for ''spring repairs.'' When the train arrives, the
baggage handlers and some of the station staff will help him load
his stuff into the baggage car. That'll probably take fifteen minutes or more, plus again that amount of time to unload it at his
destination. Yet, his fare and express charges combined didn't
amount to much more than ten dollars. That's what you call a
people-oriented railroad—or else, a labor-intensive one, if you're
an economist! Either way, it's a fact that this wilderness passen-
ger-train service is losing lots of money each year, some paid by
the ACR, the rest by the federal government, which provides
general subsidies because the train provides ''vital services.''

Finally, we're underway: ''Fifty-two cars of mixed freight,''
says the conductor, with two diesel engines somewhere up ahead.
Our train stretches through the yard and around a bend, so that
we can't even see the head end from back here. It must be entering
the main line about now. Wonder how close behind that passenger
train is? Oh well, it'll stop a while here at the station, which will
give us time to get further north. Louis Mozzonello says we'll
let them pass us in Oba.

There's a long, low gondola right ahead of our van, partly
filled with big steel plates from the mill at the Soo. We're lucky
not to have a boxcar up ahead; they really restrict the forward
view, even up here from the cupola. We're now out on the main
line, but the front of the train has already disappeared around
another curve, so we still haven't seen it. For all we know, all
these cars could be runaways, us following innocently behind.
But, if we look back at the crews in their steel van behind us,
we'll know that their radio says everything is all right.

Seventy-five pounds of air pressure shows in the gauge mounted
on the wall beside me. It wavers up and down, as the engineer
applies the train's brakes and then lets them off. If the gauge

goes down too low, we won't be able to stop. The brakemen aren't able to climb over the train, as in the past, to tighten handbrakes on the cars. They still have those brakes, but the roofwalks were removed after laws eliminated them because they were dangerous.

It's dark and we've reached our destination already. Even on a slow freight train, the time can go by quickly. After my last notes in here, we pulled into a siding at Franz to let the southbound freight go by, then we made a dash for Oba, getting into the siding there just minutes ahead of the passenger train—one engine and three cars—which stirred up the snow as it passed. We photographed it while our engine and crew did some switching on the side tracks. At Oba, the ACR's tracks cross the trans-Canada main line of the Canadian National Railway, so the two frequently exchange cars.

We're parked near the station at Hearst, Ontario, a two-story wooden structure that looms over the small yard. There used to be another CN trans-Canada main line coming through here, with both railroads sharing this station. But, just lately, much of the CN track beyond Hearst was abandoned, so that now the place is more important as a final destination for ACR trains than as a transcontinental connection. After our crew left for their hotel rooms "in town," (they used to live aboard their vans here), we were left alone in the yard, with the depot closed up tight and seemingly deserted.

Okan offered to cook the lake trout while I busied myself with tripod and camera, taking time exposures on the theme of "the old wooden caboose at the terminal." First, Okan helped me light the two kerosene marker lamps, which we then hung outside on their brackets, making sure they were turned so that red showed to the back, green to the sides and front. "Putting up the markers" is an old railroad tradition dying out slightly faster, even, than cabooses. Modern steel vans generally have electric "tail lights" permanently "put up."

A steady snowfall added drama to my night photography. It

was illuminated by station lights in the background. Between them and our van sat the day's passenger train, dark and empty like the building, waiting to head back south early in the morning. Eerie signs of life, the clouds of steam rose from its heating pipes into the night sky between us and the station lights, creating fantastic moving patterns.

After an hour of stomping my feet to keep warm and holding a gloved hand over the camera, while keeping the shutter patiently open, it was a sublime feeling to come in here where it's warm and cozy and find that Okan had made an excellent meal. He'd set the table so sumptuously that I could have taken a good photo promoting fine caboose dining, if there were a market for such a thing. He'd embellished the meal with a few treats from our luggage, including a batch of chocolate cookies. Outside our windows, the snowflakes kept swirling down through the light and steam.

Next morning, 9 A.M.: We are backing away from the station through the small Hearst yard, waving goodbye to Willie B. Taylor and Walter Wesley, who are standing beside the tracks. They asked me to mention their names in my book; so there you are, fellows! You're a couple of hardy and interesting men, that's for sure. Even the train crew seems kind of awed by your fortitude.

Walter lives right near the tracks down in a little frozen swamp of willow and birch trees. His home? One of those green folding tents that hardware stores sell for family use in summertime. Walter has put some plyboards around it to keep out the worst blasts of winter; often, it's twenty or thirty below. There's no heater, just an open fire out front that would consume the tent long before it would ever warm up its occupants.

Willie's "just in town for the weekend," he told us, staying with his old friend Walter. He's a pretty spunky old guy for being well into his seventies, sleeping out in a frozen slough with just a few blankets and a thin tent. He's got a log cabin of his own,

along his trapline, "about sixty miles south, out in the bush,"
he said.

We're some miles down from Hearst and just passed a place
called Horsey, which looks anything but—no stable, barn, corral
or riding trail. Maybe somebody got lost here once and yelled
themselves horsey? These imaginative Northlanders!

There was a little section house at Horsey, left from an era
when the ACR was even more people oriented (and labor inten-
sive) than it is now, supporting groups of track workers in little
places like Horsey every few miles along the line. Like most of
the section houses we've seen, this one was locked up, its windows boarded. By the front door was an imposing metal "No.
7," as if a mailman might need this identification in making his
rounds—though the one building in isolated Horsey shouldn't be
too hard to identify.

Rattle, rattle; clatter, clatter; clunkety-clunk; there's a constant din of noises as we roll right along at about thirty-five miles
per hour. Doesn't sound like a fast speed, but it seems different
when you're constantly bucking—up and down, sideways, sometimes kind of round and round—in an endless shimmy.

It's still snowing; big flakes, gently drifting down, gently
until they hit the trail of turbulence caused by our passing. Those
that reach our windows melt instantly from the warmth. There
is a timelessness about them, especially as seen from our peculiar,
high-up environment.

We've got a visitor! Peter Domich came in here as we pulled
away from the last siding, saying, "I'll ride up with you fellows
for a while." Peter is the rear brakeman on this train; normally
he'd be the conductor, but Louis has more seniority.

"When we lived on the road in our vans," he said in a
commanding voice, "I always carried along my shotgun; I was
a great one for hunting. Used to tuck my shells right along here."
He pointed to a shell-width gap between the air-gauge pipes and

the cupola wall. "Twelve gauge, singleshot; I used it for birds: partridge, ducks, geese. Mostly I shot partridges, usually when we were out on work trains, sitting still in one place for a long time, traveling along slowly. I'd see them from up here, shoot two or three of them, then cook them on our stove. We had pot-bellied coalburners in the vans then, not these little propane ones like you've got here.

"I'd skin the birds in the sink and clean them, then put them in a pot with half a cup of water, along with some onions, celery, salt and pepper. I parboiled them; just kept adding a little water until they were done right. The juice made good gravy, especially when I cooked up some potatoes to go with the birds. I can't think of a finer meal.

"I used to shoot moose from the train, too. That was years ago, when the pace of railroading was slower and more relaxed. Sometimes we'd be out on the line for weeks with a work train, repairing bridges and tracks. The fresh meat made a good change for our meals.

"Best place to shoot moose used to be from up on the front platform of the engine. We'd know pretty well where to keep our eyes open for moose, once hunting season started, since we went up and down nearly every day. If I shot one, we'd stop the train long enough for me to take a knife and ax and quarter it, so I could load it up on the engine's running boards. Usually everyone in the crew got a share of the meat. I was glad when we had to quit this sport, because I got tired of doing all the work with the animal by myself, only to give half of it away afterwards. Some of the fellows didn't want anything to do with it until it came time to go home with a chunk.

"Twenty minutes from the time I shot one, I'd have it quart-ered and loaded up. We've always run on train-order schedules here [one of the few mainline railroads that still do so], so we could easily make up our lost time before the next station.

"I've been on some work trains where we lived in our van for a month at a time. Of course, that could get pretty crowded and uncomfortable, four men together, spending so long in one of *these*. The worst part was the sleeping. Some guy would go out and get drunk, then come back to his bunk, just a-burping and a-farting, stinking the place up. It'd drive you crazy! Especially if it was a hot night and you had an upper bunk. Then there was the mosquitoes, and those little tiny black flies, to add misery. Boy, I tell you, there was times I wondered if I'd survive!

"Back in those days the vans were usually assigned to a conductor; some men had theirs for many years. Most of these old conductors got to be pretty proud of their vans; they'd have curtains on the windows and lots of other little homey things. Some conductors wouldn't let anyone into their vans except their own crew men, and their word was law. They never let them look grubby, like this one is now. You can tell that it hasn't been assigned in years; windows are too dirty; the walls are too stained.

"I worked with conductors who kept doormats in their vans and made the trainmen wipe their feet before entering. We'd mop the floor about every day; clean the lamps and windows; fill up our water and coal; empty the stove's ashes. We always carried spare grub, in case we got stuck somewhere. Bedding and blankets were standard equipment. The conductors even had tickets along with their paperwork; if a passenger was stranded out on the line and there was no passenger train coming, we'd sell them a ticket to ride in the van. Traveling salesmen rode with us quite a bit, going from one little place to the next."

Until the mid-seventies there were nothing but wooden vans on the ACR, (although it was the first major Canadian railroad to dieselize, in 1952). Then, train crews went on strike; among a number of issues was the demand for newer and better-equipped *steel* cabooses.

"The company offered to rebuild these wooden ones, put in electricity, better heating, better riding, and so forth," said Peter, shaking his head sadly, "but we turned them down. Biggest mistake we ever made! We were much better off with these."

And what about the calls of nature, when your train is merrily rolling along and your caboose has no toilet? Well, for simple calls the solution is equally simple: Stand out on the back plat-

form, aim rearward and watch that you don't fall. Look out for
the back-draft, too! For more serious needs, a shovel was taken
out back, a rag or newspaper placed on it, which was afterward
flung out into the bushes. "It took some doing to squat and
balance at the same time out there," said Peter convincingly.

It is now autumn 1987. Okan and I went back home for a
busy spring and summer. After crossing and recrossing the coun-
try aboard *The Canadian* and heading in and out of our Caboose
Camp in the Rockies, we now find ourselves once more aboard
ACR van 9517. We wanted to do some documenting during the
ACR's beautiful "fall foliage" season.

The air in Sault Sainte Marie is frosty this morning. As they
pass under the viaduct, automobiles show their exhaust beneath
our tracks. We're parked in the ACR Steelton yard, at the edge
of the "Great Lakes industrial world," sitting right on top of this
busy viaduct. We slept here all night, ready to head north early
this morning on the back of a wayfreight. What a spot for holding
a reunion with a wilderness caboose!

Our main sight from up in the cupola, looking beyond the
maze of yard tracks, is the steaming, smoke-spewing skyline of
the Algoma Steel Company's huge mill. Like an oozing boil, it
stands out; yet, it is the lifeline supporting most of the region's
residents, including all the railway workers. Without it, they
would be unable to live here, for the nearby wilderness could
not sustain them.

If you're fortunate enough to live along the ACR and you
have an l.c.l. shipment (that's *less-than-car*load freight), this is
the day you want to send it. Our train is No. 9, the monthly
wayfreight (weekly in summer) that will stop *anywhere* to drop
off *anything*, from a roll of barbed wire, a dog house or a snow-
machine, to all the lumber and supplies you need for a new cabin.

We've made arrangements to ride up to Hawk Junction with
No. 9 to document its journey. Since van No. 9517 was sitting
idle, Superintendent Mills had it put on this train for us. The
crew will be busy enough today inside their own van, which is

steel car No. 9603, without having to avoid two photographers. There are twenty-four loads coupled ahead of us, led by a set of four maroon-, yellow- and grey-painted diesels. It's a very nice-looking train, as far as modern freights go.

A few minutes ago, Conductor Gerry Knox stopped by to say hello (we've ridden with him on other trips), and I asked if there was much work for today's crew. Said he: "We've got *lots* of work!" I thought perhaps most of it would be done up front, close to the engines, but it turns out all the l.c.l. freight will be unloaded from two boxcars back here, directly in front of us, thus close enough to photograph. Added the conductor, with a mischievous grin, "Since you're closer, I was figuring to have *you* do the unloading while *I* take pictures!"

We're all set to go, but we're waiting in the Steelton yard for the two passenger trains to head out, first. The tour train was supposed to have gone long ago, but they developed car troubles. That's a major problem for the ACR's passenger services—all the cars are vintage forties and fifties, good equipment when new, but now needing frequent repairs with hard-to-get parts. New cars run into the millions of dollars—costs that a wilderness railroad cannot justify in these times.

If your own financial situation is much stronger than the ACR's, how about helping out the railway by chartering one of the most glamorous train trips available anywhere? For only $4,000, *you* (and up to a dozen friends or family members) can take a two-day round-trip along the ACR's main line aboard the 1913-built official car "Agawa" or the equally luxurious 1910-built "Michipicoten." A personal attendant will serve meals and drinks, making your party feel like railroading royalty. Many have made such a trip their "vacation of a lifetime."

Conductor Knox says the "Agawa" is on the back of the tour train today. He knows because his wife is the new attendant, having recently taken over from the man who looked after these two cars for nearly forty years. Today's outing is the last private charter of the season, a one-day round-trip to Agawa Canyon. . . . They just rolled past us on the main line, in fact. The conductor waved to his wife, who stepped outside briefly to join some of her guests on their car's brass-railed, rear platform.

At last, we're away from the industrial yard and several miles out of the city. It doesn't take long to reach the wilderness on this railroad (though some would say that a place with three trains rolling through within a couple of hours could hardly be classified as wild). The two passenger trains are up ahead of us; we won't see them again until they turn and head back down.

Trout Lake is our first stop, according to the signboard back along the tracks. A pretty little lake, quiet, surrounded by a forest of green pines and yellow leaves. There's a little cabin sitting in a clearing just back from the tracks; we seem to be coming to a stop in front of it. The door is standing open; there's smoke rising from a chimney; a little shed beside it is filled with chopped firewood.

Looking out of my opened cupola window, I see a husky, middle-aged man, dressed in a plaid shirt like a lumberjack, looking expectantly toward our crew. They are walking up from their van, at the rear. There are friendly greetings—they all obviously know each other—then the clank of a steel boxcar door being opened. Here comes the first item: a silver-painted tank of propane.

Thud! It falls to the grassy ground. Thud! goes another one. Then clank and clatter, as a third one is shoved out the boxcar door only to fall onto the first two. Okan and I look at each other with concern! Two more bottles are tossed out, and we know they are full! [The crewmen told us later that they've never heard of a dropped bottle exploding. We're still not convinced.]

We've got a three-man crew on the van, instead of the usual two (or, as on most main lines now, just one, *when* they have a caboose). The extra crewman is Kelly Ross, our "jump man." Why jump? Because his job is to *jump* in and out of those two boxcars all day long, unloading the l.c.l. goods. Not an easy job, which is why he's youngest on the seniority roster.

"Now I'm all set to go bird hunting," called the woodsman,

as we pulled away from Trout Lake, leaving him alone, standing amidst propane bottles, groceries and a pile of new lumber. The conductor says guys like him stay alone for a month or two at a time, shooting wild birds and catching fish, enjoying their lives of solitude. Visitors, groceries and mail come in by train; the visitors go out the same way, *when* they want to.

Sitting still on a siding, out in peaceful nowhere. Batchawana, it's called, same as the winding river that flows alongside. Betcha nobody much lives here, either, except for fish and moose and such.

The southbound tour train is due to pass at any moment, heading back to the Soo with its load of passengers. They've already been up to fabulous Agawa Canyon and taken a two-hour break for picnics, resting and hiking, while we're still trundling along way behind them.

The Agawa Canyon tour train (the *Wilderness Train*) has become the ACR's top attraction, with seats regularly selling out. Its twenty-six cars and four diesel locomotives make it among the longest regularly scheduled trains running in North America. This is a money-making train, carrying no baggage and making no intermediate stops. Up to two thousand passengers make the canyon trip on a good day. By contrast, the railway's regular passenger train is lucky to carry that many people in a week, though many of them require special stops that cost in crew time, fuel and equipment wear.

The twenty-minute wait here, on the Batchawana siding, got us so relaxed that, a few minutes ago, the tour train quietly glided past us without our getting a single photo of it. It's kind of a tight spot, anyway, with us right alongside the main line, the Batchawana River beyond that. Not much place to hop around with cameras!

The name of this place reminded our conductor that Peter Nadjiwon, our head-end brakeman (riding up front with the engineer) is an Ojibwa Indian from the Batchawana Reserve. He's even an elected member of the governing band-council, whose duties he manages to intertwine with railroading. We've heard of people with Native American ancestry in just about every part of ACR operations, another of the line's distinctions.

Said our red-haired conductor at one point: "Geez, I've got a train *full* of Indians today!" His rear brakeman, Alfie Skouris, is also of Ojibwa ancestry, although he was raised away from the reserve and has only recently received legal Indian status— since the Canadian government changed the laws that, for years, had automatically removed such status from Indian women who married non-Indian men and then kept it from the resulting children.

A contrast to the Native American Canadians on the crew is our young engineer, Dave Prior, who hails from England. His skill at the throttle and brake is European precise; crew members rate him ahead of engineers nearly twice his age and seniority. So far, we haven't had one rough jolt back here in our van, in spite of all the stopping and going. A while ago, I had a full cup of water at my lips when we moved away from a stop, with not one drop being spilled. That is very good for a wooden van on a freight train!

Pulling away from another siding: We just now got rid of most of the l.c.l. goods that had remained on board, nearly a boxcar load of building supplies—lumber, batts of insulation, sacks of cement, concrete blocks and so forth.

Four husky fellows waited for the load with a homemade trailer pulled by a sturdy tractor whose wheels were chained for navigating the local mud roads. They were a bunch of neighbors, living way out here in the wilds, anxious to build winter additions to their cabins with the supplies. One bearded, long-haired fellow said he was an artist and seemed eager for appreciative company. During our brief meeting—while he was doing his share of the unloading—he invited Okan and me to come back for a longer stay, saying, "I'm *always* here; this is where I find all the subjects I need for painting!"

*   *   *

Following morning, after spending the night parked again in the yard at Hawk Junction: It feels good to be back here, to see that nothing has changed. We got in late last night, after the slow trip up here. The last work we did out on the road was to pick up an occupied work train from a siding where repair work had just been completed. The work crew was having supper in their dining car (an old one of 1930s vintage); Okan was cooking supper for us in here; one of the train crew was doing the same back in their van. Then the work train cook sent a present—two apple pies, hot from his oven. As our engines pulled the work train from the siding, we waved our thanks, and the cook waved back from his car's open doorway, his white hat and apron standing out in the evening light.

We just had a visit from "Fernie" Thomas, Hawk Junction's regular trainmaster, who came to verify our travel plans. Another old caboose hand, Fernie began on the ACR in the late steam era as a brakeman. He not only arranged for us to bring this van for a trip over the Michipicoten Harbour branch today, but made sure the van would be put on the tail end for one part of the trip, thus making it the train's official rear and requiring that the marker lamps be properly "hung out." When we get to the end of the branch, this will eliminate the need for the two cabooses to be switched.

"Branch line to the Moon," that's what the ACR should call this. What a stark contrast to the scenery along the main line, especially down at Agawa Canyon, only a few miles away. Instead of unspoiled wilderness, nature here has been smothered almost to death. For most of this century a string of ore-processing plants along here have spewed out pollutants that poisoned the wilderness all around. For miles, the train tracks have been running amidst barren rocks and boulders, with little lakes sparkling amongst them here and there, but with none of the tall, dense trees and bush that grew here in abundance less than one hundred years ago.

One S-curve follows the next, as we wind our way sometimes right, sometimes left, at the same time always going up and down. Using the telephoto lens on my camera to focus up ahead feels like watching a model train wind through an oddly concocted miniature landscape. If someone modeled this scenery on his layout, viewers would say it doesn't look real.

Now there is greenery growing again among these polluted boulders, lakes and hills—small stuff, which the crew says is coming back to life lately because only one smelter remains open, and it is under strict environmental control. Nature is being given a chance to reclaim its own . . .

This is a tough dilemma for ACR families, many of whom depend on nature for a form of ''sustenance therapy,'' in which they hunt, fish and grow more of their own food than the employees of any other railroad that we know of. Their most famous train brings tourists from all over the world to enjoy a company-owned wilderness park. Yet, a major source of freight revenue is responsible for causing unquestionable harm to the outdoor environment.

The threat of closure hangs in the air beneath the two huge stacks at the Wawa smelter; its closure would mean the end for this forty-one-mile branch and its lucrative traffic. Along the way, we've seen the remains of other plants—with rotting ties, and the weedgrown roadbeds of former sidings and spurs—and even a large cleared area where the ACR once had an important freight yard and roundhouse.

We switched cars for quite a while at the smelter, awed by its immensity, slightly depressed by its seeming lack of humans. We didn't see anyone other than our train crew and a railroad section gang in hard hats repairing a siding. Since then, we've come another eleven miles, parked now just a few hundred yards from the end of the track.

The two vans are coupled together, sitting on a windy bluff overlooking Michipicoten Harbour. It's lunchtime on this scenic inlet of Lake Superior. Okan is downstairs fixing ours; the crew brought theirs in lunch pails. After lunch will come the second half of our branchline trip, heading back to Hawk Junction with the loads.

We've got a pretty harmonious crew—three of them are Hawk Junction relatives—and the pace on the branch seems more relaxing, since there are no other trains. The Conductor is Cliff Bain, our fisherman friend's portly and jovial father. Head-end brakeman is Billy Bain, who is Kenny's brother, while our engineer is their brother-in-law. Wrote the elder Bain for my notes: "The Father, the Son, and the Holy Ghost."

It's hard to imagine the windblown chunk of land between us and the water as having once been the site of a busy seaside community. Superintendent Mills grew up here, at a time when ACR passenger trains rolled up to the docks and met Great Lakes steamers. Just one dock remains, visited by occasional ships bringing ore for the Wawa smelter; today, our train will carry a load of it. With no ship there now, nor any buildings remaining near it, the old dock looks depressingly lonely on this windy day. If the smelter shuts down, business days at Michipicoten Harbour will be over completely; peaceful nature will get back its scenic bay.

We're still aboard the van, but this time parked where scenic nature has always reigned supreme, in the fabulous Agawa Canyon. Each one of the cupola windows frames a different, idyllic scene: At center, three sets of shiny tracks stream out from underneath us, fading away into the forested distance. To the right, steep, rocky walls of the canyon are covered so thickly with vegetation that we cannot see the high waterfalls among them. To the left, some distance below the railroad grade, flows the Agawa River, smoothly here, rapidly at other spots, a busy route for trout, beaver, otter, moose and more. Right here, the ACR truly lives "in harmony with nature." This is one important reason why Okan and I favor train travel and rail transport.

The van is parked on what's called the "house track." Next to it is a long passing siding and then the main line, both of which are used daily. Since breakfast, we've seen three passenger trains, two freights and a line of small-wheeled, slow-moving track repair equipment. That's not counting the little, yellow, four-wheeled car that the canyon park staff push up and down the house track after the passenger trains leave, collecting bags of tourist garbage dropped off by train crews.

Imagine a freight-hauling railroad keeping part of its own land base as a wilderness park, then bringing people out on its trains so that they can enjoy the wild scenery. They stay long enough to view several highlights, but not so long as to get out and disturb any of it. There are no camping facilities, no motels; only the sounds of nature, five minutes after the trains have gone.

This evening Okan and I were mesmerized by a large otter who put on a fantastic performance near the shore of the river, less than fifty feet from where a thousand people had passed a few hours earlier. For half an hour this otter played coy with us, swimming near then suddenly diving, coming back up further away, but with both eyes still on us, occasionally making sounds like the purring of a big cat.

Okan is out on the river right now, paddling a small canoe, checking to see what the local speckled trout think of his Hawk Junction worms. We gathered them by flashlight, the other night, on the rain-soaked lawn beside the station. There are several good fish pools nearby.

Here in the canyon, the sun goes away much earlier than the actual daylight, leaving everything bathed for a time in near twilight. The last time Okan and I experienced this phenomenon was several miles down in the Grand Canyon, a few years ago, after we hiked in to visit an isolated Indian village. Like that place, this canyon is also an ancient sacred ground, though there has been no Indian village here for a long, long time.

There are several rustic park buildings, however, all painted a matching dark brown, with white trim. Chief of these is the two-story park office, sitting at trackside and looking very much like the Agawa Canyon Station, though this place does not have an official station. In place of an agent, it has a park ranger, Rick

Vosper, with an official uniform and appropriate school degrees, though he was born and raised just a few miles down the line at Frater, where his father was the station agent (and where Rick still lives with his wife, when not on summer park duty).

We've been a novelty to Ranger Rick's park staff, "camped" here in our caboose, since none of them have lived along a railroad like the ACR. For Rick, our passing is only the most recent of unusual situations. He recalled that the ACR used to get rid of bothersome beavers (those who insisted on building dams that flooded the line) by hauling an old trapper up and down in a specially assigned van. Years ago, the ACR used to rent out wooden bunk cars to members of the "Group of Seven" (famous Canadian artists) who lived and painted in them at various ACR locations, including right here at Agawa Canyon.

One long ring—three turns on the crank—got me connected by wall phone at the canyon park office to the station operator at Hawk Junction.

"Hawk," said a distant-sounding voice at the other end of the crackly line.

"This is Canyon," I said loudly, hoping my talk would be carried acceptably by this lonely wilderness wire.

"Hello Canyon," came the cheerful reply. "What can I do for you?"

I asked what time he expected No. 10 to get here and pick us up, headed for the Soo.

"They left here late, so I doubt that they'll be there before twenty-two-thirty. Don't worry, they've got the orders to lift your van from the house track."

And so we waited until just an hour before midnight, when we finally heard the distant rumbling of wheels and heavy motors coming down the canyon. A speck of light grew ever larger as the head end approached, until the bright headlights themselves came into view and rounded the bend up ahead, illuminating ribbons of rail and adjacent buildings, the quaint park office standing out as an impressive silhouette. We felt humbled, inside this van, by the knowledge that six big locomotives and fifty-four cars of freight were being brought to a halt just to retrieve us from our siding.

Rather than backing up to us with the whole train, on the curving tracks and at night, the crew uncoupled the engines and did the work with them, hooking us on just ahead of their own steel van. "Are you two ready to go," called the conductor up to us, before giving a highball to the engineer over their radio.

So here I am, up in the cupola, writing by moonlight! The moon is full tonight, so that I can actually read the notes on my lap. It just came up over the horizon a few minutes ago, bright and clear, prompting me to write these final few lines. Okan is already asleep in his bunk, and I was heading there myself when I noticed the outdoors suddenly becoming very light.

It has been a *long* day for us; too soon, an even longer one will begin. We should arrive in the ACR's main Steelton yard before daybreak, though it's been arranged that we don't have to disembark right away. Later we'll make our way to Sault Sainte Marie's airport, where a local flight will bring us to Toronto, to be followed by a cross-country flight to Calgary. There, some of our family will be waiting with our truck for the drive across the Rockies. By tomorrow at this time we should be back home, aboard our *own* cabooses!

Fifty-four car roofs are shining up ahead, curving and twisting their way through the night. The lights from the engines are mostly hidden from my view, except when the landscape opens up long enough for me to see that far ahead. From back here, the course of our journey seems vague; we trust our lives fully to the engineer, or else to the One who is making him function so efficiently. Back here I cannot even hear the whine of the big motors.

"Clickety-clack, clickety-clack, clickety-clack. Kerr-thump, kerr-thump, kerr-thump. Kerr-thump, kerr-thump, kerr-thump." All the old-time sounds of train travel are here. These are un-welded rails—not like the *big* main lines—so the wheels still strike a constant array of joints. Combined with all the squeaks, groans and rattles, it amazes me that this old car has survived such strenuous travel for over fifty years. It seems that at any moment a big chunk of it could fall off or break; our wooden box could be torn asunder, with us and everything in it scattered through the moonlit countryside.

And what a view I have of that big, beautiful, pale-yellow orb; greetings to a lifelong friend, an elder in our family. Its light is like a blessing being bestowed upon the very end of this fascinating caboose journey. A dazzling light and a double dose of it, half of it reflected up from the long, narrow lake along whose shores we are now rolling. The moon's double image is only broken by a thin black band made up of the opposite shore of the lake, topped by the jagged silhouettes of pine-covered ridges.

Somewhere out in that broad scene, I'm sure there is a moose, or else a black bear or a pack of timber wolves; all of them are common along here. Right now, they may have paused in their trails, perked up their ears and listened to our train's passing. I've seen wild animals doing just that, at home, when freight trains pass up and down our valley. After the last echoes of our van's rumbling wheels have faded away, somewhere along this lake the wild animals will continue with their travels. Perhaps that band of wolves will howl, while I pretend I hear them. . . .

To obtain a list of railway books,
video programs and photo products
by Adolf and Okan Hungry Wolf, write:

GOOD MEDICINE BOOKS
Box 844
Skookumchuck, BC
CANADA V0B 2E0